THE WHOLE HEALTH
COOKBOOK

COLE ADAM, RD • CHEF KAYLA GRANTHAM • AUSTIN JOSEPH

YOUR DELICIOUS
GUIDE TO HEALTHY
**PLANT-BASED
EATING**

Printed in the United States of America

First Printing 2019

ISBN: 978-1-54399-357-8

Whole Health Club
5856 S Lowell Blvd #24
Littleton, CO 80123

Wholehealthclub.com

The information presented in this book is true complete to the best of our knowledge and according to the scientific data used to formulate this guide. This book is intended as a guide for those interested in learning more about plant-based eating and improving their health and is not intended to diagnose, treat, or cure any specific condition. The information in this book is intended for the general public and the authors and Whole Health Club do not make any guarantees of its efficacy, safety, or usefulness for any specific individual. The information in this book is not intended to contradict or replace guidance provided to you by your physician, and the ultimate decision to change your diet and lifestyle is yours. Individuals interested in changing their diet or lifestyle should consult with a physician, Registered Dietitian Nutritionist (RDN), or other qualified professional.

Many of the designations used by manufacturers and sellers to distinguish their products are claimed as trademarks. Where those designations appear in this book and Whole Health Club and the authors were aware of a trademark claim, they are printed with initial capital letters.

table of contents

GETTING STARTED

SAUCES

BREAKFAST

SIMPLE MEALS

FAMILY MEALS

SOUPS

SNACKS

SMOOTHIES

ABOUT THE AUTHORS

CHEF KAYLA GRANTHAM is a classically trained chef with a Culinary Arts degree from Johnson and Wales University. After several years working in plant-based kitchens, she joined the Whole Health Club team to create the world's first gym with an onsite teaching kitchen. Kayla designed Whole Health Club's cooking curriculum and meal plans, helping clients regain their health and learn that healthy cooking can taste even better than their old go-to's. In 2019, Kayla accepted a position in the Culinary School at Johnson and Wales University and works daily to help aspiring chefs achieve their dreams.

COLE ADAM, RDN is a Registered Dietitian with a degree in nutrition science from the University of Wisconsin. An avid hiker, photographer, gardener, and cook, Cole shares his love of plant-based food and nutrition through his popular blog, Eat Wild Greens. Cole currently works in an intensive cardiac rehab program, counseling heart attack survivors and using lifestyle interventions to help patients reverse chronic disease.

AUSTIN JOSEPH is Whole Health Club's nutritionist and general manager. After graduating from Colorado State University with a degree in Nutrition and Dietetics, they helped design Whole Health Club's signature meal plan. This widely-praised plan has helped clients drop thousands of unwanted pounds and points on their cholesterol, and has allowed people to achieve goals they thought were far out of reach. A published fiction author and animal-lover, Austin can often be found working on a new book with a dog or cat on their lap.

Whole Health Club is the world's first gym with an onsite teaching kitchen. Founded in 2016 by Chef Kayla Grantham, Sam Grantham, Chase Parker, and Paige Parker, Whole Health Club uses evidence-based nutrition practices and lifestyle interventions to help clients take back their health, fight disease, and live longer. As one of the fastest-growing gyms in Denver, Colorado, Whole Health Club has the opportunity to impact large segments of the population. Our mission is simple: we want to eliminate the chronic diseases that can be prevented through lifestyle change by helping as many people as possible to make that change.

We've printed the very best of what we do with our clients in this book. We want to share what we've learned and help you improve your health and change your life.

We would like to acknowledge a few very important individuals and extend our thanks to them: Sam Grantham, for putting this team together and pushing us to pursue this dream. Koltar Martin, for the beautiful cover design. Without your help, this book would not have been possible.

getting started

This book is for *you.* That means we want you to use it however it will benefit you best. If you want to read the in-depth articles and learn new things, go for it! If you don't care about any of that and you just want to eat your way through the recipes, you can do that and *still* end up healthier. At the end of the day, a whole food, plant-based diet will benefit you whether or not you know all the facts behind it. Our mission is to make you healthier, so if you don't want to worry about all the details, you don't need to! Just eat plants and everything else will fall into place.

WHY PLANT-BASED?

COLE ADAM, RD

"Let food be thy medicine and medicine be thy food."
–Hippocrates

There is a general consensus among unbiased nutrition experts that the best diet for human health is one made of mostly unprocessed, plant-based foods. This way of eating is commonly referred to as a "whole food, plant-based" (WFPB) diet. When broken down, "plant-based" means a diet centered on plants, and "whole food" means those plants should be consumed in their whole, naturally-occurring, and minimally processed state. For example, on a WFPB diet, we eat fruit, not Fruit Loops; corn, not high-fructose corn syrup; brown rice, not rice crispy treats.

Although similar to a vegetarian or vegan diet in that it avoids animal products, WFPB goes a step further by emphasizing the consumption of fruits, vegetables, whole grains, legumes, nuts, and seeds while limiting or avoiding animal products and highly processed foods such as added oils, refined grains, and artificial sweeteners.

Research clearly and consistently points to a WFPB diet as the best option for the prevention, treatment, and sometimes reversal of our most common chronic diseases. You can see the referenced pages for more details and specific references on each fact:

- This lifestyle is associated with the lowest rates of cardiovascular disease and cardiovascular risk factors such as high blood pressure, high cholesterol, and inflammation. It is also the only diet proven to reverse heart disease (see more on page 114).[1]
- A WFPB diet is the best way to lower our risk of type 2 diabetes, and can be used to treat or even reverse type 2 diabetes in those who already have it (see more on page 136)
- The American Cancer Society recommends adopting a plant-based diet for cancer prevention, as it can significantly lower our overall cancer risk and appears especially protective against cancers of the breast, prostate, and colon (see more on page 173).
- A WFPB diet can prevent and even slow the progression of dementia, including Alzheimer's disease (see more on page 116).

A WFPB diet is also one of the healthiest dietary strategies for weight loss and weight maintenance, and the list of medical conditions that can be improved with plant-based nutrition continues to grow. Gastric reflux, gout, Crohn's disease, erectile dysfunction, stroke, fatty liver disease, kidney stones, gallstones, and macular degeneration all seem to benefit from a WFPB lifestyle.[2-10]

What's good for us is also good for the planet

Animal agriculture is a leading source of greenhouse gas emissions, which fuel climate change. It is also a leading cause of deforestation, loss of biodiversity and native wild-life, and requires massive amounts of resources including fresh water, land, and fossil fuels.[11] The world's appetite for animal products is also responsible for the slaughter of roughly 150 billion animals each year. By adopting a plant-based diet, we can shrink our environmental footprint, live a more compassionate life, and know that we're benefiting ourselves and others.

In short, we recommend a WFPB diet for optimal health, a clean planet, and compassion toward all beings. Plus, as you'll see from the recipes in this book, WFPB tastes amazing! All the flavors and textures the Earth has to offer are ours for eating.

BLUE ZONES

AUSTIN JOSEPH, WHOLE HEALTH CLUB NUTRITIONIST

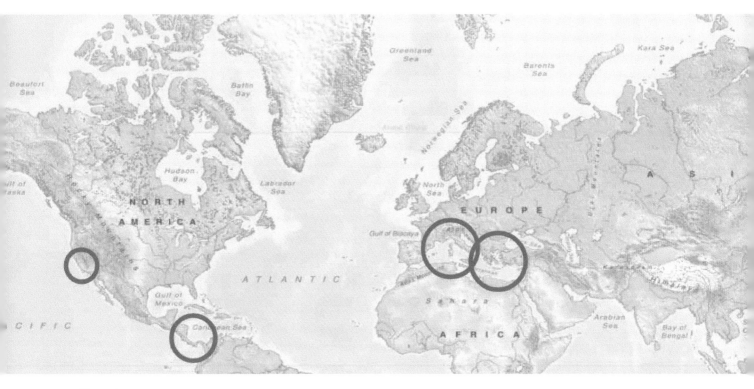

Mapswire.com

Some of the most convincing evidence for the benefits of a whole foods, plant-based diet comes from "Blue Zones." Simply put, Blue Zones are areas where people live longer, named for the blue circles researchers Gianni Pes and Michel Poulain drew on a map of Sardinia, Italy. Researcher Dan Buettner later built on their work and identified four additional areas where people live longer. He coined the term "Blue Zones" to describe these locations, which are Loma Linda, California; Okinawa, Japan; Nicoya, Costa Rica; Ikaria, Greece and the original Sardinia, Italy.[12]

Through their research, the Blue Zones team identified several factors each of these five regions had in common. Among these factors is a lifelong habit of eating unprocessed plant foods like fruits, vegetables, whole grains, and legumes. In fact, the Blue

Zones team recommends eating 95-100% plant-based.[13] People in all Blue Zones consume less meat, dairy, and eggs than the average American, and a large number of the Loma Linda Blue Zone's residents do not consume any meat.[14]

At Whole Health Club, our mission is to help people live longer, healthier lives. Learning how to do that means learning from the people who already live the longest! People living in Blue Zones take a holistic approach to health, centering healthy relationships with family and friends, regular exercise, a sense of purpose, and healthy eating. If you want to live a longer, healthier life, take a cue from the people living in Blue Zones!

GROCERY SHOPPING

CHEF KAYLA

With so many different products and brands sitting on the shelves, the grocery store can be an intimidating place. Some people enjoy taking the time to go through each aisle to find new products, but most people don't have the time for that. I'm here to bring you some tips and tricks to help make grocery shopping quick, simple, and maybe even a little fun.

When navigating the grocery store, it's important to stay on the outside of the aisles (near the produce section). After all, most of the food you buy should be produce! Try and buy seasonal fruit and vegetables. They will be higher quality and will most likely be the cheapest.

When in the aisles, stick to spices, condiments, whole grains, plant based milks and specialty items like tofu or nutritional yeast. This will make your trip to the store way faster. If you find certain brands you love, get those every time you shop so you already know what you're going in for.

Making lists can also help make your trip faster. I like using my phone to make a list so I don't have to keep track of a separate notebook or piece of paper. Here are a few important staple items to always get when grocery shopping. You'll use these most days you're in the kitchen.

- Fruits, vegetables, whole grains, beans, and other legumes
- Vegetable broth
- Almond milk or other plant-based milk
- Seasonings like coconut aminos, liquid aminos, dijon mustard, lemons, garlic, vinegar, and dry spices
- Sweeteners like maple syrup or dates.

Be sure to read the ingredients before you buy or eat anything. You may be surprised what fillers, animal products, and other unhealthy ingredients can wind up in food. For a quick check, you can use the spot at the end of the ingredient list that says "contains or may contain". This makes it easy to see if there is dairy, eggs, soy, or nuts in the product. Don't worry too much about the "may contain"—that's for allergy purposes. It just means the product was made on equipment that also handled dairy or eggs, so "may contain" is okay to buy!

KITCHEN TOOLS, UTENSILS AND EQUIPMENT MUST-HAVES

CHEF KAYLA

Having the right tools will make cooking efficient and easy for you. It can be an investment, but we recommend having the following tools to make your time in the kitchen faster and more effective. We consider the first few absolutely essential:

Chef's knife—used almost every time you make something! Keeping it sharp is very important because a dull knife can slow you down and increases the risk of getting cut.

Wooden spoon—great for mixing things in pots or pans. Sturdy and will get the job done right.

High speed blender—a lot of the recipes and sauces in this book call for a high speed blender, so it will be helpful to invest in a nice one. A few of our favorites are Vitamix, Ninja, and Blendtec.

The rest of the following items aren't absolutely essential, but will definitely improve your cooking ability and kitchen experience. Many are already found in most kitchens, but if you don't have them, consider finding them in the store. Start small and work your way up from there—don't get overwhelmed if you're missing a lot from this list!

Cutting, Chopping, and Slicing

- Cutting board
- Food processor—small & large
- Paring Knife
- Peeler
- Serrated knife
- Spiralizer
- Zester

Mixing, Stirring, and Serving

- Ladle
- Mixing bowls
- Slotted spoon
- Spatula—flat flip
- Spatula—rubber
- Tongs
- Whisk
- Wok

Pots and Pans

- Boiling pot
- Baking sheets
- Glass baking dishes
- Saucepan
- Sauté pan
- Silicone baking mats

Other Useful Tools and Appliances

- Can opener
- Lemon squeezer
- Prep container/bowls
- Rice cooker
- Strainer
- Toaster

STOCKING YOUR PANTRY

CHEF KAYLA

Pexels/Pixabay

Mise en place originated from French cuisine. It basically means having everything you need prepped and ready to go before you ever start cooking. We recommend setting out all the ingredients for the recipe you are creating and setting out all pots, pans, baking sheets, knives, utensils and appliances that you will use while you cook.

It's also always important to have a stocked kitchen. Here is a list of must-haves that you'll be using almost every time you cook recipes from this book. Keeping these ingredients stocked in your pantry at all times will help make cooking more fun and convenient.

- Garlic—cloves or pre-minced garlic (1 garlic clove=½ tbsp. minced garlic)
- Onions—red, white, yellow, green
- Vinegars—white vinegar, apple cider vinegar, balsamic vinegar
- Condiments—yellow mustard, Dijon, ketchup, hot sauce, BBQ sauce, miso paste, tahini, liquid smoke, coconut aminos, liquid aminos
- Non-dairy milk of choice—almond, soy, oat, hemp, cashew, pea
- Nuts/seeds—cashews, almonds, walnuts, pecans, chia seeds, flaxseeds, hemp seeds, sunflower seeds, pumpkin seeds
- Spices—paprika, black pepper, oregano, basil, garlic powder, onion powder, cumin, chili powder, thyme, rosemary, smoked paprika, curry, turmeric, ginger powder
- Vegetable broth—low sodium only
- Cans of tomatoes—crushed, diced, whole

- Cans of beans—pinto, black, garbanzo/chickpeas, kidney (be sure these are "low sodium" or "no salt added")
- Protein powder—plant based only! Not necessary but nice to have on hand to throw in date balls, oatmeal and smoothies.
- Nutritional yeast
- Dates
- Maple syrup
- Whole wheat flour
- Lemons

OIL-FREE COOKING—WHAT??

AUSTIN JOSEPH, WHOLE HEALTH CLUB NUTRITIONIST

Oil is in everything. It's in processed foods and unhealthy recipes like cakes, sure, but you can also find oil in most of the supposedly healthy recipes out there. Part of this is because oil is just ingrained in cooking. We use oil because we've always used oil. It's useful to prevent sticking, it's necessary for frying, and our bodies are programmed to crave fat. The idea of cooking without oil can be daunting for even experienced cooks, and would be laughed at by most "serious" (if ill-informed) chefs.

Buissinne/Pixabay

We've also been told for a long time that certain oils like olive oil are healthy. But these claims are largely conjecture, based on information extrapolated from studies about the Mediterranean diet.

The Mediterranean diet *does* include large amounts of olive oil. Given what we know about oil though, it seems unlikely that olive oil itself is actually responsible for the Mediterranean diet's health benefits. Studies show that high fat consumption (including fat from olive oil) impairs the function of the cells lining our blood vessels.[15] We know that high fat consumption contributes to heart disease and diabetes, and that at four *thousand* calories per pound, oil is one of the most calorically dense foods available. In addition to all that, we at Whole Health Club have seen some amazing weight loss results when clients start cooking without oil. That's why we choose to avoid it.

This book will teach you how to cook your food with vegetable broth instead of oil (see the next page for this) and how to make dressings and sauces from whole fats that retain the nutritional benefits oils have lost.

BROTH OR WATER SAUTÉING AND ROASTING

Chef Kayla

Cooking without oil can be a little confusing at first, but only because we've been taught that it's essential. Most recipes, cooking shows, and people we know accept it as a given that oil will be used. However, I'm here to tell you that you don't need *any* type of oil to cook your plant-based recipes.

If you've flipped ahead in the book, you may have noticed that most of the recipes don't call for any type of cooking oil. You'll see sesame oil in a few, but that's just a small addition for flavor rather than for cooking. You may be asking yourself how you can possibly cook without any oil. The answer is to use vegetable broth or water! It's that simple, and I promise it works just as well. By cooking without oil, we can get the same results without adding unnecessary fat to our food.

How to sauté without oil:
1. Place your pan on the stove and turn on the heat
2. Add a splash of vegetable broth or water in the bottom of the pan before adding any other items. (Use a little more than you would if you were using oil)
3. Stir your food more often than you would if you were cooking with oil— we need to stir regularly to prevent food from sticking and get it cooked evenly!
4. If the broth or water cooks off before your items are done cooking, just add more! The great thing is that if you add too much, you can just turn up the heat a bit and give it time to cook off.

How to roast without oil:

1. Line your pan or baking sheet with parchment paper or silicone baking mats to prevent sticking.
2. Place your food on the parchment paper or silicone baking mats and cook it in the oven just like you normally would!

In addition to reducing the calorie and fat content of our meals, this technique doesn't leave your pans covered in oil residue, so cleanup is much easier. Happy oil-free cooking!

CHIPOTLE
DRESSING

YIELD: 2 CUPS | COOK TIME: 5 MINUTES

INGREDIENTS:

1 CUP ALMONDS, SOAKED 4-6 HOURS
½ TBSP. APPLE CIDER VINEGAR
½ LEMON, JUICED
1 TBSP. GARLIC, MINCED
½ OR 1 FULL CAN CHIPOTLE PEPPERS IN ADOBO SAUCE
½ CUP LOW-SODIUM VEGETABLE BROTH
¼ CUP ALMOND MILK
½ CUP NUTRITIONAL YEAST

DIRECTIONS:

1. Combine all ingredients in a high speed blender. Only add ½ can chipotle peppers if you don't want the sauce to be too spicy. For more spice, add the full can.

2. Blend until smooth. Slowly add more vegetable broth to make sauce thinner and smoother until preferred texture is reached.

    Tip: Try with Potato Nachos (pictured on previous page). You can find them on page 71!

C A S H E W
CHEESE

YIELD: 2 CUPS | COOK TIME: 5 MINUTES

INGREDIENTS:

1 CUP CASHEWS
½ CUP NUTRITIONAL YEAST
1 TBSP. DIJON MUSTARD
1 TBSP. LIQUID AMINOS
1 TBSP. GARLIC, MINCED
1 LEMON, JUICED (CAN SUB 1 TBSP. APPLE CIDER VINEGAR IF PREFERRED)
2 TSP. BLACK PEPPER
½ CUP LOW-SODIUM VEGETABLE BROTH OR MORE TO THIN SAUCE

DIRECTIONS:

1. Place all ingredients in a high speed blender.

2. Blend until smooth. Add more vegetable broth or water to make sauce thinner and smoother until preferred texture is reached.

MISO GINGER
TAHINI DRESSING

YIELD: 2 CUPS | COOK TIME: 5 MINUTES

INGREDIENTS:

1 CUP TAHINI

1 TBSP. GARLIC, MINCED

1 TBSP. LIQUID AMINOS

1 TBSP. FRESH MINCED GINGER OR 1 TBSP. GINGER POWDER

2 TSP. SESAME OIL

2 TBSP. MISO PASTE

½ CUP WATER

1 LIME, JUICED

1 TBSP. MAPLE SYRUP

1 TSP. BLACK PEPPER

DIRECTIONS:

1. Add all ingredients to a high speed blender.

2. Blend sauce until smooth. Taste and adjust seasoning according to preference.

PEANUT
SAUCE

YIELD: 2 CUPS | COOK TIME: 5 MINUTES

INGREDIENTS:

1 CUP NATURAL PEANUT BUTTER

¼ CUP LIQUID AMINOS

⅓ CUP COCONUT AMINOS

1 TBSP. GARLIC, MINCED

1 TBSP. RICE VINEGAR

1 TBSP. MAPLE SYRUP

2 TSP. SESAME OIL

2 TSP. GINGER POWDER

2 TSP. CHILI GARLIC SAUCE

½ CUP WATER

DIRECTIONS:

1. Place all ingredients except water in a medium saucepan.

2. Cook on low heat until peanut butter melts, stirring occasionally.

3. Bring to a simmer and add the water, continuing to stir. Once sauce thickens, remove from heat.

Tip: add to Soba Noodle Bowl (pictured on previous page). You can find it on page 79!

WHITE BEAN **TURMERIC DRESSING**

YIELD: 2 CUPS | COOK TIME: 5 MINUTES

INGREDIENTS:

1 CAN WHITE BEANS

1 TBSP. APPLE CIDER VINEGAR OR 1 WHOLE LEMON, JUICED

½ CUP NUTRITIONAL YEAST

1 TBSP. GARLIC

2 TSP. TURMERIC

2 TSP. THYME

2 TSP. BASIL

2 TSP. SAGE

1 TSP. BLACK PEPPER

1 TBSP. LIQUID AMINOS

½ TO ¾ CUPS LOW-SODIUM VEGETABLE BROTH

DIRECTIONS:

1. Add all ingredients to a high speed blender and blend until smooth.

WALNUT **BALSAMIC DRESSING**

YIELD: 2 CUPS | COOK TIME: 5 MINUTES

INGREDIENTS:

1 CUP WALNUTS

2 GARLIC CLOVES

1 TBSP. COCONUT AMINOS

2 TSP. MAPLE SYRUP

1 TBSP. DIJON MUSTARD

1 TBSP. THYME, DRIED OR FRESH

1 TBSP. ROSEMARY, DRIED OR FRESH

1 TBSP. BASIL, DRIED OR FRESH

½ CUP BALSAMIC VINEGAR

1 TBSP. NUTRITIONAL YEAST

½ CUP WATER OR LOW-SODIUM VEGETABLE BROTH

DIRECTIONS:

1. Place all ingredients in a high speed blender and blend until smooth.

MUSHROOM
GRAVY

YIELD: 2 CUPS | COOK TIME: 10 MINUTES

INGREDIENTS:

2 CUPS WHITE BUTTON MUSHROOMS, CHOPPED

3 CUPS LOW-SODIUM VEGETABLE BROTH + 2 TBSP. MORE FOR SAUTÉING

1 YELLOW ONION, SMALL DICED

3 LARGE GARLIC CLOVES, MINCED

1 TBSP. LIQUID AMINOS

2 TSP. DRIED THYME

2 TSP. DRIED ROSEMARY

2 TSP. DRIED SAGE

2 TSP. BLACK PEPPER

2 TBSP. CORNSTARCH

½ CUP WATER

2 TSP. RED WINE VINEGAR

DIRECTIONS:

1. Start by adding 2 tbsp. vegetable broth, diced onions, and garlic to a large skillet or sauté pan. Cook until onions are translucent. Deglaze pan with red wine vinegar (add in red wine vinegar while pan is still hot, allowing the liquid to pull up flavors that may have cooked onto the pan).

2. Add in chopped mushrooms and cook for 5 minutes until mushrooms are soft.

3. Add in all spices, liquid aminos, and remaining vegetable broth. Mix well.

4. Create a slurry by adding water to cornstarch. Stir slowly with a spoon or whisk. Add slurry to pan.

5. Cook on low heat until gravy starts to thicken, then turn off heat.

6. Taste and adjust seasoning if needed.

N A C H O
CHEESE

YIELD: 2 CUPS | COOK TIME: 10 MINUTES

INGREDIENTS:

1 CUP CASHEWS, SOAKED 4-6 HOURS
3 LARGE YUKON GOLD POTATOES, CHOPPED
2 LARGE CARROTS, CHOPPED
1 MEDIUM ONION, CHOPPED
¾ CUP NUTRITIONAL YEAST
4 GARLIC CLOVES, MINCED
¾ TO 1 CUP WATER
2 TSP. CHILI POWDER
1 ½ TBSP. APPLE CIDER VINEGAR OR 1 WHOLE LEMON, JUICED
1 TBSP. LIQUID AMINOS

DIRECTIONS:

1. Bring a large pot of water to boil. Add potatoes, carrots, and onions to the pot and boil until soft.

2. Combine cashews, nutritional yeast, garlic, water, chili powder, apple cider vinegar (or lemon juice), and liquid aminos in a high speed blender. Blend until smooth. If needed, you can add some of the water from the cooking vegetables to thin the sauce.

3. Once potatoes, carrots, and onions are soft, add them to the blender. Blend until smooth. Add water or vegetable broth to thin sauce if needed.

STIR FRY **CHILI SAUCE**

YIELD: 1 CUP | COOK TIME: 5 MINUTES

INGREDIENTS:

½ CUP VEGETABLE BROTH

2 TBSP. LIQUID OR COCONUT AMINOS

¼ CUP NUTRITIONAL YEAST

3 GARLIC CLOVES, MINCED

2 TBSP. GINGER POWDER

1-2 TBSP. RED PEPPER FLAKES

DIRECTIONS:

1. Using a spoon, mix all ingredients together in a small bowl.

2. Chill in the fridge for 3-4 hours to thicken (sauce will remain fairly thin even after chilling and is best poured over rice or another grain that can absorb it)

BBQ **SAUCE**

YIELD: 2 CUPS | COOK TIME: 5 MINUTES

INGREDIENTS:

1 CAN TOMATO SAUCE

1 CAN TOMATO PASTE

⅓ CUP APPLE CIDER VINEGAR

¼ CUP MAPLE SYRUP

¼ CUP PURE BLACKSTRAP MOLASSES

2 TBSP. WORCESTERSHIRE SAUCE

2 TSP. LIQUID SMOKE

2 TSP. PAPRIKA

2 TSP. SMOKED PAPRIKA

2 TSP. MUSTARD POWDER

1 TSP. GARLIC POWDER

1 TSP. ONION POWDER

1 TSP. BLACK PEPPER

WATER TO THIN OUT SAUCE

DIRECTIONS:

1. Add all ingredients to a saucepan and stir together until everything is mixed well.

2. Cook on low heat for 20 minutes, stirring occasionally.

3. If the sauce is too thick, add water in 1 tbsp. increments and stir to thin.

   Tip: use on cauliflower wings (pictured on previous page). You can find them on page 80!

breakfast

CLASSIC
OATMEAL

YIELD: 1-2 SERVINGS | COOK TIME: 10 MINUTES

INGREDIENTS:

1 CUP ROLLED OATS
2 CUPS WATER
1 TBSP. GROUND FLAXSEED
FRESH FRUIT FOR TOPPING
SPLASH OF PLANT-BASED MILK (OPTIONAL)

DIRECTIONS:

1. Place the rolled oats, ground flaxseed, and water in a microwave-safe bowl and stir.

2. Place the bowl in the microwave and heat for 2-3 minutes or until the oats start to thicken.

3. Remove from microwave, add an optional splash of plant-based milk, and stir until creamy. If it's too dry, add more plant-based milk or water. If it's too wet, place it back in the microwave for 30-second increments until the desired consistency is reached.

4. Top with fruit of choice. Berries and sliced bananas or diced apples with cinnamon go great with oatmeal.

QUINOA SWEET
POTATO BOWL

YIELD: 1 BOWL | COOK TIME: 10 MINUTES

INGREDIENTS:

½ CUP QUINOA, COOKED
1 SWEET POTATO, MASHED
2 TBSP. NUT BUTTER (PEANUT, ALMOND, OR CASHEW)
⅔ CUP ALMOND MILK
1 TBSP. GROUND FLAXSEED
1 TBSP. HEMP SEEDS
2 TSP. CINNAMON
2 TSP. VANILLA EXTRACT
TOPPINGS: SUNFLOWER SEEDS, DRIED FRUIT, COCOA NIBS, GRANOLA

DIRECTIONS:

1. Slice sweet potatoes into half-inch thick circles, leaving the skin on.

2. Place sweet potato slices in a pot and fill with water. Boil until potatoes are soft enough to mash.

3. Once sweet potatoes are soft, drain the water and peel the skin off each potato.

4. Mash with a fork. Season with a splash of almond milk, vanilla, cinnamon, and black pepper.

5. Add cooked quinoa to a bowl and place the mashed sweet potato on top.

6. Cover with nut butter, seeds, and toppings.

LOADED TOFU
SCRAMBLE

YIELD: 4-5 SERVINGS | COOK TIME: 45 MINUTES

INGREDIENTS:

2 BLOCKS TOFU, DRAINED AND PRESSED
2 TBSP. TURMERIC
1 ½ TBSP. NUTRITIONAL YEAST
1 TSP. GARLIC POWDER
1 TSP. ONION POWDER
1 TSP. CHILI POWDER
½ TSP. BLACK PEPPER
1 SWEET POTATO, SMALL DICED
1 YUKON GOLD POTATO, SMALL DICED
½ RED BELL PEPPER, MINCED
½ ONION, MINCED
2 GARLIC CLOVES, MINCED
1 CUP MUSHROOMS, DE-STEMMED AND CHOPPED
(SHIITAKE, WHITE BUTTON, OR CREMINI ARE BEST)
1 YELLOW SQUASH, DICED
1 GREEN ZUCCHINI, DICED IN HALF-INCH CUBES
1 CUP FRESH OR FROZEN SPINACH, CHOPPED

DIRECTIONS:

1. Rinse the tofu blocks, then wrap them in a dish towel or paper towel and press hard to remove excess liquid. Crumble the tofu into scrambled egg-size pieces in a bowl.

2. Add the turmeric, nutritional yeast, garlic powder, onion powder, chili powder, and black pepper to tofu. Mix until the tofu is evenly coated with spices. Set aside.

3. In a nonstick skillet over medium-high heat, add the chopped potato, onion, bell pepper, and ¼ cup of water. Sauté for 10 minutes.

4. Add garlic, zucchini, mushrooms, and spinach. Sauté for another 5 minutes or until potatoes are close to their desired tenderness.

5. Add the tofu/spice mixture. Stir well and continue to sauté for an additional 5 minutes or until all veggies have cooked properly.

6. Garnish with avocado and hot sauce. Serve with whole-grain toast and a side of fruit.

BREAKFAST
BURRITO

YIELD: 2-3 BURRITOS | COOK TIME: 65 MINUTES

INGREDIENTS:

2-3 WHOLE WHEAT FLOUR TORTILLAS
1 CUP POTATOES, DICED & BLANCHED UNTIL SOFT
1 CUP BROWN RICE, COOKED
½ CUP SPINACH
TOFU SCRAMBLE (SEE RECIPE ON PREVIOUS PAGE)
HOT SAUCE OR SALSA TO TASTE

DIRECTIONS:

1. Assemble burritos by scooping cooked potatoes, brown rice, tofu scramble and spinach onto the whole wheat tortillas.

2. Wrap burritos by folding the tortilla over the filling, then fold in the sides and roll tightly to the edge of the tortilla, tucking as you roll.

3. If desired, add hot sauce or salsa on top.

CHOCOLATE CHIA
SEED PUDDING

YIELD: 2-4 SERVINGS | COOK TIME: 3-8 HOURS OR OVERNIGHT

INGREDIENTS:

½ CUP CHIA SEEDS
2 CUPS UNSWEETENED PLANT-BASED MILK
4 DATES, PITTED
3 TBSP. CACAO POWDER
1 ½ TSP. VANILLA EXTRACT
1 BANANA, SLICED (OPTIONAL)
CACAO NIBS TO TASTE (OPTIONAL)
PEANUT BUTTER TO TASTE (OPTIONAL)
STRAWBERRIES TO TASTE (OPTIONAL)
RASPBERRIES TO TASTE (OPTIONAL)

DIRECTIONS:

1. Add the dates, milk, cacao, and vanilla to a blender and blend until smooth.

2. Pour the blended mixture into a medium-sized mixing bowl.

3. Add the chia seeds and stir until they are evenly mixed and immersed in the liquid.

4. Refrigerate overnight or for at least 3 hours.

5. Serve cold and top with sliced bananas and cacao nibs.

6. Add additional toppings such as raspberries, diced strawberries, or a dollop of peanut butter.

P O T A T O
H A S H

YIELD: 2-4 SERVINGS | COOK TIME: 30 MINUTES

INGREDIENTS:

4 CUPS POTATOES, PEELED AND DICED
¼ CUP VEGETABLE BROTH + MORE FOR SAUTÉING
1 GREEN BELL PEPPER, DICED
1 CARROT, PEELED AND DICED
1 ONION, DICED
3 GARLIC CLOVES, MINCED
1 TBSP. OREGANO
1 TBSP. THYME
2 TSP. BASIL
2 TSP. PAPRIKA
1 TSP. BLACK PEPPER

DIRECTIONS:

1. Place diced potatoes on a baking sheet and cover with ¼ cup of veggie broth and all the spices. Mix together until potatoes are evenly coated in spices.

2. Bake at 425 degrees Fahrenheit for 20 minutes or until brown and crispy on the outside.

3. Sauté onion, bell pepper, and garlic in a splash of vegetable broth.

4. Once the veggies are soft, add the roasted potatoes in with the veggies.

5. Mix together until ingredients are evenly distributed. Adjust seasoning if needed.

CHICKPEA FLOUR
OMELETTE

YIELD: 2-3 OMELETTES | COOK TIME: 15 MINUTES

INGREDIENTS:

BATTER:
1 CUP CHICKPEA FLOUR
1 CUP WATER
1 TBSP. GARLIC POWDER
1 TBSP. ONION POWDER
1 TBSP. TURMERIC
2 TBSP. NUTRITIONAL YEAST
2 TSP. BLACK PEPPER

TOPPINGS:
½ CUP MUSHROOMS, CHOPPED
¼ CUP FRESH SPINACH
1 ROMA TOMATO, DICED
1 AVOCADO
HOT SAUCE TO TASTE
SALSA TO TASTE

DIRECTIONS:

1. Mix batter ingredients together in a bowl. Continue mixing until there are no lumps.

2. Heat a medium skillet on medium-high heat and pour about ½ cup batter on the skillet. Spin the pan to spread the batter out.

3. Add toppings. When the edges of the omelette start to cook, flip it over (like a pancake). It should take 2-3 minutes for each side.

4. Serve with hot sauce, salsa and avocado.

BREAKFAST
SANDWICH

YIELD: 2-3 SANDWICHES | COOK TIME: 55 MINUTES

INGREDIENTS:

4-6 PIECES OF BREAD OR 2-3 BAGELS OR BISCUITS OF CHOICE

1 CHICKPEA FLOUR OMELETTE PATTY (SEE RECIPE ON PREVIOUS PAGE)

1 BLOCK TEMPEH, THINLY SLICED

3 TBSP. COCONUT AMINOS

1 TSP. GARLIC POWDER

1 TBSP. SMOKED PAPRIKA

1 TSP. LIQUID SMOKE

1 TSP. BLACK PEPPER

¼ CUP CASHEW CHEESE (SEE RECIPE ON PAGE 14)

3 PIECES OF LETTUCE OF CHOICE (ROMAINE, SPINACH, ARUGULA)

1 TOMATO, SLICED

½ RED ONION, SLICED

HOT SAUCE OR SALSA

DIRECTIONS:

1. Preheat oven to 400 degrees Fahrenheit.

2. Combine coconut aminos, garlic powder, smoked paprika, liquid smoke, and black pepper in a bowl to create a marinade.

3. Place sliced tempeh in the bottom of the bowl and cover with marinade.

4. Once tempeh is coated, place on a baking sheet.

5. Bake for 20 minutes or until crispy on top and edges.

6. Toast bread and add cashew cheese on one slice.

7. Assemble sandwiches by stacking the chickpea omelettes, tempeh bacon, lettuce, tomato, onion, and hot sauce between slices of toasted bread.

HOMEMADE
GRANOLA

YIELD: 1 LARGE MASON JAR | COOK TIME: 30 MINUTES

INGREDIENTS:

1 CUP ALMONDS

1 CUP GOJI BERRIES

1 CUP WALNUTS

1 CUP CASHEWS

1 CUP DRIED CRANBERRIES OR ANY DRIED FRUIT OF YOUR CHOICE

½ CUP HEMP SEEDS

1 TBSP. CHIA MEAL

1 CUP QUICK OATS

1 TBSP. GROUND FLAXSEED

10 DATES, PITTED AND CHOPPED

1 CUP COCONUT FLAKES OR SHREDDED COCONUT

4 TBSP. PURE MAPLE SYRUP

1 TBSP. CINNAMON

1 ½ TBSP. VANILLA

1 TSP. NUTMEG

½ CUP SUNFLOWER SEEDS

½ CUP PUMPKIN SEEDS

DIRECTIONS:

1. Preheat oven to 375 degrees Fahrenheit.

2. Mix all dry ingredients together in a bowl.

3. In a separate bowl, mix wet ingredients together. Pour over dry ingredients and mix thoroughly.

4. Spread granola mixture over a baking sheet lined with parchment or a silicone baking mat.

5. Bake for 20-25 minutes or until nuts start to brown.

6. Cool and place in a sealed container.

OVERNIGHT
OATS

YIELD: 1-2 SERVINGS | COOK TIME: OVERNIGHT

INGREDIENTS:

1 CUP ROLLED OATS
1 CUP UNSWEETENED PLANT-BASED MILK
1 TBSP. CHIA SEEDS
½ TSP. CINNAMON
½ TSP. VANILLA EXTRACT
1 CUP FRESH OR FROZEN BERRIES

DIRECTIONS:

1. Add the oats, chia seeds, cinnamon, vanilla, and plant-based milk to a medium-sized mason jar or other glass container. Stir well.

2. Top with fresh or frozen berries.

3. Cover and refrigerate overnight or for at least two hours.

4. Enjoy cold the next morning. If the overnight oats are too thick after refrigeration, add more milk. If they're too thin, add more chia seeds and let them soak for at least 10 minutes.

FRENCH
TOAST

YIELD: 2-4 PIECES OF TOAST | COOK TIME: 20-25 MINUTES

INGREDIENTS:

½ CUP WHOLE WHEAT FLOUR

¼ TSP. BAKING POWDER

½ TSP. CINNAMON

½ TSP. NUTMEG

1 TBSP. PURE MAPLE SYRUP

2 CUPS UNSWEETENED PLANT-BASED MILK

1 TSP. VANILLA

10 SLICES OF DAY-OLD SOURDOUGH BREAD

DIRECTIONS:

1. Mix dry ingredients (except bread) together in a bowl

2. Next, add the wet ingredients (except maple syrup). Whisk until everything is combined.

3. Warm a large sauté pan on medium-high heat.

4. Dunk 1 piece of sourdough into batter, coating both sides evenly. Shake off excess liquid. Lay flat in hot pan and cook on both sides for 3-4 minutes until golden brown.

5. Top with maple syrup and fresh fruit.

WHAT ABOUT CARBS?
ISN'T FRUIT TOO SUGARY?

AUSTIN JOSEPH, WHOLE HEALTH CLUB NUTRITIONIST

After years of bombardment from carb-hating proponents of fad diets, a lot of people have started believing we should limit our consumption of fruit, starchy veggies like potatoes, and whole grains. However, doing this deprives us of some of the healthiest foods available. Fruits, starchy veggies, and whole grains contain countless nutrients that are beneficial and even vital to human health, *including* carbohydrates!

That's right, carbs are good for us! There's a common saying in weight loss nutrition: "fat burns in a carbohydrate flame." This is due to a complex series of reactions that take place in fat metabolism. In short, pyruvate (a product of carbohydrate metabolism) must be available in the mitochondria for us to break down fat for energy. Without carbohydrates available, fat metabolism stalls until the body begins breaking down protein for pyruvate. So we need our "carbohydrate flame" to burn fat in the most efficient possible way! Beyond that, carbohydrates help preserve muscle mass and help us feel full. They're also the body's preferred energy source, meaning that a carbohydrate-rich diet will give you more energy for exercise and everyday activities.

Sure, but what about sugar? While table sugar is certainly something to stay away from, it turns out that the sugar in fruit is nothing to be afraid of. As Dr. Michael Greger of Nutritionfacts.org explains, the fiber and phytonutrients naturally found in fruit actually have a stabilizing effect on blood sugar.[16] In a study published in the Journal of Nutrition, researchers had volunteers consume white and rye bread with or without pureed berries on the side. Participants' blood sugar was then measured after the bread was consumed. Participants who ate bread alone showed a large spike and crash in blood sugar (normal after eating something like plain bread). However, participants who added berries showed a smaller rise in blood sugar even though they were technically consuming more sugar than the first group.[17] This is because fruit contains fiber and polyphenols that mitigate the blood sugar response. So when consumed as part of a whole fruit, fruit sugars behave differently in the body than table sugar does.

Fruit, starchy veggies, and whole grains all contain valuable vitamins, minerals, and phytonutrients that improve heart health, fight inflammation, promote immune function, and prevent cancer cell growth (see our All About Phytochemicals article on page 172 for more info on this). And as we saw during our discussion on Blue Zones, people eating diets high in these food groups tend to live longer. So make sure to eat your fruits, starchy veggies, and whole grains!

COMMON NUTRIENT QUESTIONS ON A PLANT-BASED DIET

COLE ADAM, RDN

Despite the abundance of evidence that indicates a plant-based diet is ideal for human health, many people fear they will miss out on certain nutrients. There are a few nutrients that require a bit more consideration, but all essential nutrients can be easily obtained on a well planned plant-based diet. Below is a list of nutrients that people often express concern about when adopting a plant-based diet. The following recommendations are for adults—nutrient needs for children, pregnant women, and those with certain medical conditions may vary.

Silvia/Pixabay

Iron: Men and postmenopausal women have much lower iron requirements than premenopausal women and can easily meet their iron needs by eating a variety of plant-based foods. Premenopausal women need to make an extra effort to consume iron-rich plant-based foods on a daily basis. These include legumes (beans, lentils, split peas, tofu, tempeh), whole grains (quinoa, barley, oats), dark leafy greens (kale, swiss chard), and seeds (sunflower, sesame, pumpkin). Consuming foods high in vitamin C can help boost the absorption of iron from plants. Bell peppers, kale, broccoli, and most fruit (especially strawberries, kiwi, oranges, and most other citrus fruit), are great sources of vitamin C. Fortified foods such as breakfast cereal, and/or supplements may need to be included if the foods mentioned above are not consumed on a regular basis.

Calcium: Most people associate calcium with dairy products. Yet humans have no more need for cow milk than we do for dog milk. In fact, much of the world's population is lactose intolerant. Where do those people get their calcium? From plants, of course! Dark leafy greens, beans, nuts, seeds, broccoli, oranges, and soy products (such as soy milk, tofu, edamame, and tempeh) are all great sources of calcium. Fortified products can also be considered, such as fortified cereals or plant-based milks.

The necessary amount of calcium for adults is between 700-900 mg per day, which can easily be achieved by eating a variety of plant-based foods. This amount is less than the U.S. nutrition guidelines (which have been inflated by the highly influential U.S dairy industry), but is reflected in the United Kingdom nutrition guidelines and the scientific literature as a whole.

Vitamin D: Few foods contain vitamin D, but we can synthesize it from the sun's UV rays. Skin tone, the latitude at which we live, and time of year all influence how much vitamin D we make from the sun. Regular, sensible sun-to-skin exposure during the summer months, can provide us with all the vitamin D we need. During the winter months, when the sun is less intense and we're mostly indoors, a vitamin D supplement or regular consumption of fortified foods such as breakfast cereals should be considered.

Omega-3 Fatty Acids: This type of fat is essential in our diet, but we only need a small amount. Regular consumption of plants rich in omega-3 can be a sufficient source for most people. These foods include walnuts, flaxseed, chia seeds, hemp seeds, mung beans, soy products, and dark leafy greens. If you've been told to take an omega-3 supplement, the preferred option would be one derived from algae (which is where fish originally get their omega-3 fatty acids), as they contain far less environmental pollutants than fish.

Protein: The idea that animal protein is "better" than plant protein is common, but incorrect. Research clearly shows that the more protein people get from plants (and less from animals), the healthier they tend to be.[18] It is also a myth that you need to combine certain plant-based foods to make a "complete" protein. All plants have protein, and when we consume a variety of plants, we will be getting all the protein we need. Good plant-based sources of protein include legumes (beans, lentils, split peas, soy products), whole grains, nuts, seeds, and even vegetables. In fact, pound for pound, spinach contains more protein than beef. Popeye was right all along!

Vitamin B12: Vitamin B12 is not made by plants or animals, but by microorganisms that blanket our natural environment. When humans lived "closer to nature," drank untreated spring water, and foraged for food, we inadvertently consumed the small amount of necessary B12. Nowadays we live in a more sterile environment, so our environmental sources of B12 are negligible. Livestock animals are fed B12 supplements, so we *could* eat animal products to obtain this vitamin. However, we'd get all the unwanted baggage that comes with consuming them, and it's easier to just get it from the same place they do: fortified foods and/or a supplement. Foods fortified with B12 include: plant-based milks, cereals, and some brands of nutritional yeast. In addition to any fortified foods, a 2,500 mcg supplement of vitamin B12 taken once a week is a smart option for anyone eating a plant-based diet. There is no toxic upper limit for B12; any excess will simply be urinated out.

simple meals

10 MINUTE
TACOS

YIELD: 2-3 TACOS | COOK TIME: 10 MINUTES

INGREDIENTS:

1 - 15OZ CAN BLACK OR PINTO BEANS, RINSED AND DRAINED

¼ RED ONION, MINCED

½ BELL PEPPER, MINCED

½ CUP SHREDDED OR CHOPPED RED CABBAGE

½ CUP LETTUCE OF CHOICE (WE LOVE ROMAINE FOR THIS ONE)

CORN TORTILLAS, LIGHTLY TOASTED IF DESIRED

1 AVOCADO, SLICED OR CHOPPED

½ CUP CILANTRO

1 LIME, JUICED

SALSA

HOT SAUCE

DIRECTIONS:

1. On a microwave safe plate, align 2-3 tortillas and top each with ¼ cup of beans.

2. Microwave for 30-45 seconds.

3. Top with desired amount of onion, pepper, cabbage, and avocado.

4. Garnish with cilantro, spritz with lime, and drizzle with salsa or hot sauce.

5. Repeat steps 1-4 until you are full!

FALL HARVEST
SALAD

YIELD: 3-4 SERVINGS | COOK TIME: 50 MINUTES

INGREDIENTS:

SALAD:

1 BUNCH ROMAINE LETTUCE, CHOPPED
1 BUNCH LACINATO (DINO) KALE, MASSAGED
AND THINLY SLICED
1 DELICATA SQUASH, SEEDED, QUARTERED
LENGTHWISE, AND CUT INTO ½-INCH SLICES
WIDTHWISE (LEAVE THE SKIN ON)
1 CUP FARRO, SOAKED FOR AT LEAST
FOUR HOURS
2 - 15OZ CANS CHICKPEAS, RINSED
AND DRAINED

1 HONEYCRISP APPLE, DICED
½ CUP DRIED CRANBERRIES
(PREFERABLY UNSWEETENED)
¼ CUP SUNFLOWER SEEDS (PREFERABLY RAW
AND UNSALTED)

DRESSING:

¾ CUP TAHINI
1 ½ TBSP. MAPLE SYRUP
3 TBSP. APPLE CIDER VINEGAR
⅓ CUP WATER (PLUS MORE TO THIN DRESSING
AS NEEDED)

DIRECTIONS:

1. Preheat oven to 400 degrees Fahrenheit.

2. Place the delicata squash pieces on a parchment-lined baking sheet and bake for 20-30 minutes or until they are tender and slightly browned on the bottoms.

3. Rinse and drain the farro grains. Add them to a small pot along with at least three cups of water and bring to a boil. Once at a boil, reduce heat to low and simmer for 30-35 minutes or until tender (they should still be slightly chewy). Remove from heat, drain off excess water, and set aside.

4. In a medium-sized mixing bowl, prepare dressing by combining the tahini, maple syrup, apple cider vinegar, and water. Whisk until evenly mixed. Add more water to thin as needed. Set aside.

5. Mix the chopped lacinato kale and romaine lettuce in a large bowl. Set aside.

6. Place chickpeas in a microwave-safe bowl. Cover with a paper towel and microwave for 90 seconds or until evenly warmed. Set aside.

7. Once everything is cooked and prepared, fill your salad bowl with mixed greens, roasted delicata squash, farro, chickpeas, diced apple, dried cranberries, and sunflower seeds. Drizzle with desired amount of dressing and enjoy!

CLASSIC PASTA WITH
VEGGIES & MARINARA

YIELD: 2-4 SERVINGS | COOK TIME: 30 MINUTES

INGREDIENTS:

1 - 16OZ PACKAGE OF WHOLE WHEAT PASTA
(ANY TYPE WILL WORK BUT WE PREFER SPAGHETTI OR PENNE)
1 GARLIC CLOVE, MINCED
½ CUP DE-STEMMED MUSHROOMS (WHITE BUTTON OR CREMINI), CHOPPED OR SLICED
½ WHITE OR YELLOW ONION, CHOPPED
1 CUP FRESH OR FROZEN SPINACH
1 - 7OZ CAN TOMATO PASTE
1 - 24OZ JAR MARINARA SAUCE
1 - 15OZ CAN CANNELLINI BEANS, RINSED AND DRAINED

DIRECTIONS:

1. Cook pasta according to package instructions.

2. While the pasta is cooking, water-sauté garlic in a large skillet over medium-low heat until garlic becomes fragrant (about 1 minute).

3. Add the mushrooms and onion. Cook for 6-8 minutes or until onions are translucent, stirring frequently.

4. Add the spinach and cook until it's wilted (or thawed, if using frozen).

5. Add the tomato paste and marinara sauce; stir well until evenly mixed.

6. Stir in beans, then reduce heat to low and simmer until the pasta is done cooking.

7. Once the pasta is cooked, drain it in a colander and add it directly to the skillet with the sauce. Stir until everything is evenly mixed, then remove from heat and serve.

THAI NOODLE
BOWL

YIELD: 3-4 BOWLS | COOK TIME: 40 MINUTES

INGREDIENTS:

NOODLES:
2 - 8OZ PACKAGES BROWN RICE PAD THAI NOODLES

6 GARLIC CLOVES, MINCED

2 TSP. FRESH GINGER, MINCED (OPTIONAL)

1 RED BELL PEPPER, JULIENNED (CUT INTO THIN STRIPS)

2 CUPS CABBAGE, CHOPPED

3 CARROTS, JULIENNED

4 STALKS BABY BOK CHOY—SEPARATE THE GREEN LEAVES FROM THE WHITE STALKS AND CHOP UP BOTH (DISCARD THE "BUTTS")

1 - 16OZ PACKAGE FROZEN SHELLED EDAMAME (REMOVE FROM FREEZER WHEN YOU START COOKING SO IT CAN THAW OUT A BIT)

FRESH LIME JUICE (OPTIONAL GARNISH)

CHOPPED CILANTRO (OPTIONAL GARNISH)

SAUCE:
½ CUP LOW-SODIUM VEGETABLE BROTH (PLUS AN ADDITIONAL ¼ CUP FOR SAUTÉING THE VEGETABLES)

6 TBSP. BROWN SUGAR

6 TBSP. LIQUID AMINOS

2-3 TBSP. CHILI GARLIC SAUCE OR SRIRACHA

3 TBSP. TAMARIND PASTE (THIS CAN BE FOUND IN THE ASIAN FOODS SECTION OF MOST GROCERY STORES)

DIRECTIONS:

1. In a large skillet over medium-high heat, add garlic, ginger, red pepper, red cabbage, carrots, chopped bok choy stalks (stalks only—we'll add the leaves later), and ¼ cup vegetable broth. Sauté, stirring frequently.

2. After about 5 minutes, add chopped bok choy leaves and edamame. Continue to stir. Cook until everything has reached desired tenderness (about 10 more minutes).

3. While the veggies are cooking, prepare the sauce by combining all sauce ingredients in a bowl and whisk until well mixed. Set aside.

4. Cook the noodles according to package instructions. Set aside.

5. Once the veggies are cooked, add the sauce to the skillet and stir well. Turn up the heat to high and cook for another minute. Then reduce heat, add the noodles, and stir until everything is evenly mixed and coated with sauce. Remove from heat.

6. Garnish with lime juice and cilantro.

BARLEY SUMMER
SALAD

YIELD: 3-4 SERVINGS | COOK TIME: 30 MINUTES

INGREDIENTS:

1 ½ CUPS DRIED HULLED BARLEY (BE SURE TO USE HULLED RATHER THAN PEARLED)

3 CUPS LOW-SODIUM VEGETABLE BROTH

2 - 15OZ CANS GARBANZO BEANS, RINSED AND DRAINED

½ CUCUMBER, DICED

¾ CUP TOMATOES, CHOPPED (ABOUT THREE MEDIUM ROMA TOMATOES)

1 CUP FRESH GREEN BEANS (OPTIONAL)

1 CUP FRESH CHOPPED FLAT-LEAF PARSLEY

2-3 TBSP. MINCED RED ONION

1 LARGE GARLIC CLOVE, MINCED

3 TBSP. CAPERS

¼ CUP KALAMATA OLIVES, SLICED

¼ CUP BANANA PEPPERS, CHOPPED

1 - 15OZ CAN ARTICHOKE HEARTS, RINSED, DRAINED, AND CHOPPED (OPTIONAL)

1 TSP. DRIED ITALIAN SEASONING (OR SUB ½ TSP. EACH OF DRIED BASIL AND OREGANO)

½ TSP. BLACK PEPPER

1 TSP. RED CHILI FLAKES

1 TBSP. RED WINE VINEGAR

1 LEMON, JUICED

DIRECTIONS:

1. Soak the barley in water for at least 30 minutes. Rinse and drain it, then add it to a pot with the vegetable broth. Bring vegetable broth to a boil, then simmer until the barley is cooked and has absorbed most of the liquid. Stir frequently, especially toward the end of cooking. The barley should be a little wet and slimy. Pour out or cook off any excess liquid.

2. While the barley is cooking, add the rest of the ingredients to a large mixing bowl.

3. Add the cooked barley, stir it all together, and enjoy!

SWEETADILLAS

YIELD: 2 SWEETADILLAS | COOK TIME: 20 MINUTES

INGREDIENTS:

4 WHOLE WHEAT FLOUR TORTILLAS (MEDIUM TO LARGE SIZE)
1 LARGE SWEET POTATO
1 CAN BLACK BEANS, DRAINED AND RINSED
2 CUPS CASHEW CHEESE (SEE RECIPE, PAGE 14)
1 AVOCADO, DICED OR MASHED
HOT SAUCE OR SALSA TO TASTE

DIRECTIONS:

1. Cut sweet potatoes into large coins, leaving skin on.

2. Place potatoes in boiling water and boil until fork-tender (about 10 minutes)

3. Once potatoes are soft enough to mash, drain out boiling water.

4. Peel skin off (this should happen easily if they are cooked all the way) and mash potatoes. Set aside.

5. Place black beans into a food processor and blend until smooth. Set aside.

6. Prepare cashew cheese in a blender (see recipe, page 14)

7. Assemble sweetadillas by spreading mashed sweet potato on one tortilla and blended black beans on the other. Drizzle cashew cheese onto one of the sides and then fit both sides together like a sandwich.

8. Cook sweetadilla in a large non-stick sauté pan on medium heat until golden brown on both sides (about 2-3 minutes per side)

9. Top with avocado and hot sauce or salsa of choice.

LEMON KALE PESTO PASTA WITH CASHEW PARMESAN

YIELD: 3-4 SERVINGS | COOK TIME: 30 MINUTES

INGREDIENTS:

PESTO PASTA:

1 - 16OZ PACKAGE WHOLE WHEAT PASTA
2-3 GARLIC CLOVES
1 BUNCH OF KALE, DE-STEMMED AND
RIPPED INTO PIECES
½ CUP LOOSELY PACKED FRESH BASIL
½ CUP HULLED HEMP SEEDS
JUICE OF TWO LEMONS
1-2 TBSP. WATER

1 - 15OZ CAN NAVY BEANS, RINSED
½ CUP SUN-DRIED TOMATOES, CHOPPED
½ TSP. BLACK PEPPER
RED PEPPER FLAKES TO TASTE
(WE USE ABOUT 1 TBSP.)

CASHEW PARMESAN (OPTIONAL):

½ CUP RAW CASHEWS
2 ½ TBSP. NUTRITIONAL YEAST
¼ TSP. GARLIC POWDER

DIRECTIONS:

1. Cook pasta according to package instructions.

2. (Optional cashew parmesan): While the pasta is cooking, add the cashews, nutritional yeast, and garlic powder to a food processor. Pulse until a coarse cornmeal consistency is reached. Pour into a bowl and set aside.

3. In the same food processor, combine garlic, lemon juice, hemp seeds, black pepper, basil, and water and process until well mixed (about 10 seconds). Add the kale and process until mixture reaches desired pesto consistency.

4. Transfer the pesto sauce to a large bowl. Add sun-dried tomatoes, red pepper flakes, and navy beans. Mix well.

5. Drain the cooked pasta and immediately add it to the bowl of pesto. Stir until pasta is evenly coated.

6. Garnish with the optional cashew parmesan and additional red pepper flakes.

FLAUTAS

YIELD: 3-4 FLAUTAS | COOK TIME: 30 MINUTES

INGREDIENTS:

5-7 WHOLE WHEAT FLOUR TORTILLAS
1 CAN BLACK BEANS, DRAINED AND RINSED
1 TBSP. CUMIN
1 TBSP. GARLIC POWDER
1 TSP. PAPRIKA
1 TSP. CHILI POWDER
1 SMALL ONION, DICED
1 CUP CASHEW CHEESE (SEE RECIPE, PAGE 14)
1 CUP SHREDDED ROMAINE LETTUCE
2 ROMA TOMATOES
1 LIME, JUICED
½ CUP CILANTRO
1 AVOCADO, DICED
HOT SAUCE OF CHOICE

DIRECTIONS:

1. Preheat oven to 400 degrees Fahrenheit.

2. Blend black beans in a blender until they form a smooth paste. Add all spices and blend for an additional 30 seconds to mix.

3. Spread black bean mixture onto tortillas. Add diced onion and cashew cheese, then roll tortilla up. Repeat until all tortillas are used.

4. Transfer flautas to a shallow baking pan and bake in the oven for 15 minutes.

5. Top with more cashew cheese, lettuce, tomato, lime juice, avocado, cilantro, and hot sauce.

MEDITERRANEAN
PIZZA

YIELD: 2 PIZZAS | COOK TIME: 10 MINUTES

INGREDIENTS:

2 WHOLE WHEAT PITA BREAD LOAVES
¼ CUP PLAIN HUMMUS
5 CHERRY TOMATOES, CUT IN HALF
¼ RED ONION, SLICED
¼ CUP KALAMATA OLIVES, CUT IN HALF
½ CUP ARUGULA
OPTIONAL TOPPINGS: CAPERS, PEPPERONCINIS, FRESH CHOPPED PARSLEY

DIRECTIONS:

1. Spread hummus evenly over the pita bread in a thin layer.

2. Top with tomatoes, olives, red onion, arugula, and any additional optional toppings.

3. Eat raw or bake at 350 degrees Fahrenheit for 10 minutes or until bread gets crispy on the edges.

CHICKPEA SALAD
SANDWICH

YIELD: 2 SANDWICHES | COOK TIME: 20 MINUTES

INGREDIENTS:

4 PIECES WHOLE WHEAT BREAD OF CHOICE
1 - 15OZ CAN CHICKPEAS, DRAINED & RINSED
2 TBSP. DIJON MUSTARD
1 TBSP. YELLOW MUSTARD
¼ CUP TAHINI
1 TBSP. DRIED DILL WEED
½ CUP CELERY, DICED
3 TBSP. CAPERS
2 GARLIC CLOVES, MINCED
2 TBSP. RED ONION, DICED
1 LEMON, JUICED
BLACK PEPPER TO TASTE

TOPPINGS:
DILL PICKLE SLICES
TOMATO, SLICED
LETTUCE OF CHOICE
RED ONION, SLICED
AVOCADO, SLICED OR MASHED
ADDITIONAL MUSTARD

DIRECTIONS:

1. In a medium mixing bowl, mash the chickpeas until there are no whole beans left.

2. Add all remaining ingredients (except toppings) and stir well, mashing as you stir.

3. Serve on whole grain bread with any of the following toppings: dill pickles, sliced tomato, lettuce, red onion, avocado, and additional mustard.

POTATO
NACHOS

YIELD: 2-3 SERVINGS | COOK TIME: 45 MINUTES

INGREDIENTS:

3-4 GOLD POTATOES
2 TSP. BLACK PEPPER
⅓ CUP LOW-SODIUM VEGETABLE BROTH
½ CAN CORN
1 CAN BLACK BEANS, DRAINED AND RINSED
½ ONION, DICED
1 GREEN BELL PEPPER, DICED
¼ CUP PURPLE CABBAGE, CHOPPED
2 GARLIC CLOVES, MINCED
¼ CUP CILANTRO
1 ROMA TOMATO, DICED
1 LIME, JUICED
2 TBSP. CHIPOTLE DRESSING (SEE RECIPE, PAGE 13)

DIRECTIONS:

1. Preheat oven to 425 degrees Fahrenheit.

2. Cut potatoes into 1-inch cubes and toss with a splash of vegetable broth and black pepper. Spread on a baking sheet lined with parchment paper or a silicone baking mat.

3. Bake potatoes for 20-25 minutes, until golden brown and crispy on the outside. Transfer to a large plate.

4. While potatoes are cooking, sauté onion, green bell pepper, cabbage, and garlic in a splash of vegetable broth.

5. Once veggies are soft, pour over top of potatoes on plate.

6. Top with corn, black beans, tomatoes, cilantro, lime juice, and chipotle dressing.

FALAFEL

YIELD: 8-10 PATTIES | COOK TIME: 35 MINUTES

INGREDIENTS:

2 - 15OZ CANS CHICKPEAS, DRAINED AND RINSED
½ ONION, CHOPPED
½ CUP PARSLEY
¼ CUP TAHINI
1 LEMON, JUICED
½ TBSP. GARLIC, MINCED
1 TSP. CUMIN
1 TSP. CARDAMOM
1 TSP. CORIANDER
1 TSP. BLACK PEPPER
1 TBSP. BAKING POWDER
1-2 CUPS OAT FLOUR

DIRECTIONS:

1. Preheat oven to 400 degrees Fahrenheit.

2. Pulse drained chickpeas, onion, parsley, tahini, and lemon juice in a blender.

3. Add minced garlic and dry spices. Blend until smooth (don't worry if there are just a few small chunks left)

4. Pour mixture into a bowl and slowly add oat flour in Ð cup increments, mixing thoroughly as you go.

5. Once mixture has a consistency thick enough to be worked on with your hands, form small patties.

6. Place patties on a baking sheet lined with parchment or a silicone baking mat.

7. Bake in the oven for 7 minutes, then flip falafel patties over and bake for 7 more minutes.

CHICKPEA CHOPPED
SALAD

YIELD: 3-4 SERVINGS | COOK TIME: 50 MINUTES

INGREDIENTS:

SALAD:
½ CUP DRY FARRO
2 MEDIUM PURPLE SWEET POTATOES (YOU CAN ALSO SUB ORANGE SWEET POTATOES)
1 HEAD ROMAINE LETTUCE, RINSED AND CHOPPED
1 BUNCH LACINATO (DINO) KALE, RINSED AND FINELY CHOPPED
½ CUP PITTED DATES, CHOPPED
½ CUP ALMONDS, CHOPPED

2 - 15OZ CANS CHICKPEAS, DRAINED AND RINSED
½ CUP UNSWEETENED DRIED CRANBERRIES

DRESSING:
¾ CUP CHAMPAGNE VINEGAR
½ CUP WATER
1 TBSP. DIJON MUSTARD
1 TBSP. MAPLE SYRUP OR AGAVE NECTAR
SALT AND PEPPER TO TASTE (OPTIONAL)

DIRECTIONS:

1. Combine farro with at least 1 cup of water in a pot and bring to a boil. Reduce heat and simmer for 25-40 minutes or until the grains are tender. Strain any excess water and set aside.

2. In a separate pot, boil enough water to submerge your sweet potatoes. Once at a boil, add the potatoes, reduce heat, and simmer for 15-20 minutes or until potatoes are tender. Remove potatoes from pot, let cool, and slice to any desired shape/size. Set aside.

3. While the farro and potatoes are cooking, prepare the dressing by whisking together the champagne vinegar, water, mustard, maple syrup, and optional salt and pepper. Set aside.

4. Chop the romaine lettuce and kale. Mix together in a large bowl and set aside.

5. Chop the almonds and dates. Set aside.

6. Assemble the salad: line a bowl with a bed of greens and top with a desired amount of farro, chickpeas, potatoes, cranberries, dates, and almonds. Drizzle dressing over salad and mix.

T A C O
SALAD

YIELD: 4 SERVINGS | COOK TIME: 45 MINUTES

INGREDIENTS:

1 CUP ROMAINE LETTUCE, WASHED & CHOPPED

½ CUP CORN (CAN BE WARM OR COLD DEPENDING ON PERSONAL PREFERENCE)

½ RED BELL PEPPER, DICED

1 CUP MUSHROOMS, CHOPPED

1 BLOCK TOFU, DRAINED AND PRESSED

1 CAN BLACK BEANS, DRAINED AND RINSED

1 CAN PINTO BEANS, DRAINED AND RINSED

¼ CUP OLIVES, SLICED

½ AVOCADO, SLICED

1 CUP CASHEW CHEESE (SEE RECIPE, PAGE 20)

1 TBSP. CUMIN

1 TBSP. ONION POWDER

1 TBSP. GARLIC POWDER

2 TSP. CHILI POWDER

2 TSP. OREGANO

2 TSP. PAPRIKA

2 TSP. BLACK PEPPER

DIRECTIONS:

1. Preheat oven to 425 degrees Fahrenheit.

2. Combine all dry spices in a small bowl. This will be your taco seasoning.

3. Crumble tofu into a bowl and add chopped mushrooms and taco seasoning. Mix together well.

4. Spread tofu mixture on a baking sheet. Bake for 15 minutes.

5. Remove tofu mixture from oven and add drained and rinsed black and pinto beans. Mix on baking sheet, then bake again for 10 more minutes or until tofu starts to brown and crisp.

6. While tofu is baking, prepare your toppings by shredding the lettuce and slicing the tomatoes, olives and avocados.

7. Prepare cashew cheese sauce (page 14)

8. Once tofu is done baking, assemble taco bowls. Start with a base of lettuce, then add tofu mixture. Top with olives, bell pepper, corn, avocado, and cashew cheese. Enjoy!

SOBA NOODLE
BOWL

YIELD: 3-5 BOWLS | COOK TIME: 55 MINUTES

INGREDIENTS:

1 PACK SOBA NOODLES
1 BLOCK TEMPEH, DRAINED AND CUBED
1 RED BELL PEPPER, SLICED
1 CUP BROCCOLI, CHOPPED
1 ONION, SLICED
1 BABY BOK CHOY, CHOPPED
½ CUP SNOW PEAS
¼ PURPLE CABBAGE, SHREDDED
1 CARROT, SLICED
2 TSP. GINGER POWDER
2 TBSP. COCONUT AMINOS
2 TSP. MINCED GARLIC
2 TSP. SESAME OIL
2 TBSP. LOW-SODIUM VEGETABLE BROTH
PEANUT SAUCE (SEE RECIPE, PAGE 17)

DIRECTIONS:

1. Preheat oven to 400 degrees Fahrenheit

2. Bring a large pot of water to a boil. Add soba noodles and cook according to package instructions (they will cook faster than most pasta)

3. While water is boiling, sauté all veggies with garlic and one-half of your ginger, vegetable broth and sesame oil. Cook until veggies are tender but still slightly crunchy.

4. Dice tempeh into cubes and marinate for twenty minutes in coconut aminos with the other half of the ginger powder, sesame oil and veggie broth.

5. Bake tempeh for 12 minutes or until brown and crispy on the sides.

6. Once noodles have cooked, drain and rinse in cold water until they are cool.

7. Assemble bowls by placing about a cup of cooked noodles in a bowl and piling veggies and tempeh on top. Toss in peanut sauce and garnish with sesame seeds.

CAULIFLOWER
WINGS

YIELD: 24-50 WINGS | COOK TIME: 50 MINUTES

INGREDIENTS:

1 HEAD CAULIFLOWER

3 CUPS BBQ SAUCE (SEE RECIPE, PAGE 23 OR USE STORE BOUGHT)

1 BOTTLE FRANK'S REDHOT SAUCE MIXED WITH ¼ CUP NUTRITIONAL YEAST

BATTER INGREDIENTS:

¾ CUP WATER

½ CUP PLANT MILK

1 CUP WHOLE WHEAT FLOUR

½ TBSP. CORN STARCH

2 TSP. GARLIC POWDER

2 TSP. ONION POWDER

2 TSP. PAPRIKA

1 TSP. BLACK PEPPER

DIRECTIONS:

1. Preheat oven to 450 degrees Fahrenheit.

2. Cut cauliflower into bite-size pieces, leaving the thickest part of the stem attached to each piece to hold the pieces together.

3. Prepare batter by combining all dry ingredients (except cauliflower and nutritional yeast) in a large bowl and all wet ingredients (except sauces) in a separate bowl. Add wet ingredients to dry ingredients and mix thoroughly until no lumps remain.

4. Dip each piece of cauliflower into the batter, coating evenly.

5. Shake off any excess batter so that only a thin layer remains on each piece of cauliflower.

6. Set cauliflower wings ½ inch apart on a baking sheet lined with parchment paper.

7. Bake for 15-20 minutes or until crispy. Remove from oven and coat with sauces of your choice.

8. Optional: after coating wings with sauce, put them back in the oven and broil for 3-7 minutes to make them extra crispy!

THE CALORIE DENSITY PRINCIPLE FOR A HEALTHY WEIGHT

AUSTIN JOSEPH, WHC NUTRITIONIST

Our bodies aren't very good at intuitively measuring calories all by themselves, so we tend to rely on (1) how much our stomachs have stretched and (2) the weight of the food in our stomachs to know how full we are. For example, eating a pound of french fries or a pound of baked potatoes will make you feel equally full—but you'll consume over four times as many calories if you pick the french fries.

This is the basis of the calorie density principle, which we use with great success at Whole Health Club. By choosing more foods that are less calorie dense, we can eat our fill, feel satisfied, and still lose weight. The principle is illustrated in the chart below.

WHC Eating Chart

Unlimited	(Calories/pound)*
Non- Starch Veggies	100
Fruits	200
Starch Veggies	350
Whole Grains	400
Beans/Lentils	500
Tofu/Tempeh	500

Moderate (3 times a week)

Pasta	600
Avocado	700
Bread	900
Nuts/Seeds	2400*

Not Recommended (0 times a week is best)

Animal Products	1200
Refined Sugar	1500
Oils	4000
Alcohol/Soda	
Processed/Fried Food	

(Approximate Values)*

Grantham, Joseph/Whole Health Club

Referencing the chart, we can see that all of our "Unlimited" food categories are under five hundred calories per pound. These are foods that make us full long before we can consume enough to gain weight from them, so we can eat as much as we want and still lose weight. As a bonus, they're the healthiest foods in the world, rich in vitamins, minerals, and disease-fighting phytochemicals (see page 172). These foods—vegetables, fruits, starches (like potatoes) whole grains (like rice or oats, not whole grain bread) legumes (beans, lentils, and peas), and soyfoods (like tofu or tempeh) should make up most of your diet!

Our "Moderate" foods such as avocado, bread, pasta, nuts, and seeds are foods that still have a place in a healthy diet, but are more calorie-dense than our green foods. We still eat these foods, and you can too! We just want to make sure these foods are eaten in moderation rather than in unlimited quantities.

Our last category on the chart—our "Not Recommended" foods—are the food groups we do our best to avoid. Not only are they significantly higher in calories and lower in nutrients than other foods, but many of them have also been linked to increased risk of disease. We advise our clients to avoid animal products (including chicken, fish, beef, pork, dairy, and eggs)as well as refined sugars (like cupcakes, cookies, ice cream, and candy), alcohol, soda, oils (see pages 9-10 for details on cooking without oil) and any refined or processed foods (tv dinners, chips, crackers, or anything else that comes from a bag).

If you're looking to lose weight or even maintain a healthy weight in a manner that's much more sustainable than the fad diets of the day, our best advice is to follow this principle. After all, we see success stories stemming from it nearly every day!

family meals

WHOLE HEALTH
TOFU STIR FRY

YIELD: 4-5 SERVINGS | COOK TIME: 45 MINUTES

INGREDIENTS:

1 BLOCK EXTRA FIRM TOFU, DRAINED AND PRESSED
3 TBSP. LIQUID AMINOS
2 TBSP. COCONUT AMINOS
3 GARLIC CLOVES, MINCED
2 TBSP. LOW-SODIUM VEGETABLE BROTH + MORE FOR COOKING IF NEEDED
1 RED BELL PEPPER, SLICED
1 HEAD BROCCOLI, CUT INTO FLORETS
1 HEAD CAULIFLOWER, CUT INTO FLORETS
1 CAN BABY CORN, DRAINED AND RINSED
2 CUPS SNOW PEAS, ENDS CUT OFF
1 ONION, SLICED

DIRECTIONS:

1. Preheat oven to 425 degrees Fahrenheit.

2. Cut tofu into half-inch cubes. Place in a bowl and cover with liquid aminos and coconut aminos.

3. Line a baking sheet with parchment paper. Arrange tofu on baking sheet, leaving a small amount of space between each cube. Bake for 20-25 minutes or until tofu is brown and crispy.

4. While the tofu is cooking, add onions, bell pepper, and garlic to a large sauté pan with a splash of vegetable broth. Cook on medium-high heat, stirring occasionally.

5. Once the onions begin to soften, add in broccoli, cauliflower, baby corn, and snow peas. Cook for 5-7 minutes or until all veggies are soft.

6. Once tofu is done, add it to the pan with the veggies and cover with stir fry chili sauce (see recipe, page 23)

STUFFED
SHELLS

YIELD: 6-8 SERVINGS | COOK TIME: 75 MINUTES

INGREDIENTS:

TWO BOXES OF EGGLESS JUMBO SHELL PASTA

2 JARS OF PASTA SAUCE (MAKE SURE IT DOESN'T HAVE ANY CHEESE HIDING IN IT!)

1 BLOCK TOFU, DRAINED AND PRESSED

½ CUP SPINACH, CHOPPED

¼ CUP ARUGULA, CHOPPED

¼ CUP CHIVES, CHOPPED

¼ CUP FRESH OREGANO, PICKED OFF STEM AND CHOPPED

¼ CUP FRESH BASIL, PICKED OFF STEM AND CHOPPED

2 CUPS RAW UNSALTED CASHEWS

1 CUP NUTRITIONAL YEAST

4 GARLIC CLOVES

1 LEMON, JUICED

¼ TSP. BLACK PEPPER

LOW-SODIUM VEGETABLE BROTH FOR BLENDING

DIRECTIONS:

1. Bring a large pot of water to boil on the stove and preheat oven to 400 degrees Fahrenheit.

2. Once water reaches a boil, cook pasta shells according to package instructions. Drain and set aside.

3. While pasta cooks, crumble tofu into fine pieces in a mixing bowl. Stir in chopped spinach, arugula, chives, oregano, and basil.

4. Prepare the cashew cheese base by combining the cashews, nutritional yeast, garlic, lemon, and black pepper in a high speed blender. Add a splash of vegetable broth and blend until smooth. Add more vegetable broth to smooth the mixture if needed, but keep in mind that the cheese base should be thick.

5. Pour cashew cheese base over tofu mixture. Mix thoroughly but gently, taking care not to smash the tofu while mixing.

6. Prepare shells by gently spooning tofu mixture into each shell, being careful to fill but not overfill or tear the shell. Line up stuffed shells in the bottom of a glass 9" x 13" pan (you can spread a few spoonfuls of pasta sauce out on the bottom of the pan first to prevent sticking).

7. Once the pan is full of shells, cover with sauce.

8. Bake in the oven for 15-20 minutes, just long enough to warm the filling all the way through (we don't want to overcook these or the pasta will get hard)

CHICKPEA KALE CURRY & **WARM FLATBREAD**

YIELD: 4 SERVINGS | COOK TIME: 40 MINUTES

INGREDIENTS:

4 GARLIC CLOVES, MINCED
1 SMALL ONION, DICED
2 CARROTS, PEELED & DICED
1 RED BELL PEPPER, DICED
1 CAN CHICKPEAS, DRAINED & RINSED
1 HEAD CAULIFLOWER, CHOPPED INTO
SMALL FLORETS
1 CUP SNOW PEAS, CHOPPED IN HALF
1 CAN DICED TOMATOES

2 CUPS KALE, WASHED & CHOPPED
4 CUPS LOW-SODIUM VEGETABLE BROTH
+ 2 TBSP. MORE FOR SAUTÉING
1 TBSP. GARAM MASALA
1 TBSP. CURRY POWDER
1 TBSP. TURMERIC
2 TSP. CUMIN
2 TSP. PAPRIKA

DIRECTIONS:

1. Heat a large pot over medium heat.
2. Add garlic, onion, carrots, red bell pepper, and 2 tbsp. vegetable broth to the bottom of the pot. Sauté until onions start to become translucent.
3. Add in chickpeas, cauliflower, snow peas, diced tomatoes, and all spices. Cook for 7-8 minutes. When cauliflower starts to soften, toss in chopped kale.
4. Add in the rest of the vegetable broth and simmer on low heat for 5 minutes.
5. Taste and adjust seasoning if needed. Serve with warm flatbread.

W A R M **FLATBREAD**

YIELD: 6-8 PIECES | COOK TIME: 15-20 MINUTES

INGREDIENTS:

1 CUP WHOLE WHEAT FLOUR
1 TBSP. BAKING POWDER

½ CUP NON-DAIRY MILK
½ CUP WATER

DIRECTIONS:

1. Mix flour and baking powder together in a bowl.
2. Add in water and non-dairy milk. Stir together until dough forms. Knead with hands until dough comes together and no lumps remain.
3. Split dough into 6-8 small balls.
4. Flour a countertop or other surface and use a rolling pin to roll out each dough ball into a flat piece of dough.
5. Heat a nonstick pan over medium heat. Toast each side of each piece of flatbread for 1-2 minutes or until golden brown.

LENTIL
SHEPHERD'S PIE

YIELD: 8-12 SERVINGS | COOK TIME: 90 MINUTES

INGREDIENTS:

MASHED POTATOES
6-7 MEDIUM YUKON GOLD
POTATOES, QUARTERED
½ TSP. GARLIC POWDER
SPLASH OF UNSWEETENED SOY MILK
(OPTIONAL)

VEGETABLE FILLING
3 GARLIC CLOVES, MINCED
1 SMALL YELLOW ONION, CHOPPED
2-3 MEDIUM CARROTS, DICED INTO PEA-
SIZED PIECES
2-3 MEDIUM CELERY RIBS, DICED INTO
PEA-SIZED PIECES

1 CUP CHOPPED WHITE BUTTON MUSHROOMS
1 CUP FROZEN GREEN PEAS
½ CUP FROZEN CHOPPED SPINACH
1 - 15OZ CAN LENTILS, RINSED AND DRAINED
(OR 15OZ COOKED LENTILS)
1 ½ CUPS VEGETABLE BROTH
¼ CUP RED WINE (OPTIONAL)
1 TBSP. DRIED THYME
½ TSP. DRIED BASIL
½ TSP. DRIED OREGANO
3 TBSP. WHOLE WHEAT FLOUR
BLACK PEPPER TO TASTE

DIRECTIONS:

Potatoes

1. In a large pot, cover potatoes with water and bring to a boil.

2. Once the water reaches a boil, reduce heat to low and simmer for 25-30 minutes or until potatoes are tender.

3. Drain the potatoes and place them back in the pot to evaporate any excess moisture.

4. Transfer potatoes to a large bowl and add garlic powder and optional splash of soy milk. Mash to desired consistency and set aside.

Vegetable Filling

1. While the potatoes are boiling, add garlic, onion, carrots, celery, mushrooms, and ¼ cup of vegetable broth to a large skillet. Sauté over medium heat for 10 minutes.

2. Stir in the frozen peas, spinach, and lentils. Sauté for another five minutes.

3. In a small bowl, whisk one cup of vegetable broth with optional red wine, thyme, basil, oregano, flour, and black pepper. Pour into skillet, reduce heat to medium-low, and mix thoroughly. Simmer until the mixture thickens (about five minutes) and set aside.

Pie

1. Preheat oven to 425 degrees Fahrenheit.

2. Add the vegetable filling to a greased 9" x 13" baking pan. Spread the veggies evenly, then top with an even layer of mashed potatoes. Garnish with a sprinkle of black pepper and paprika and place in the oven.

3. Bake for 35 minutes or until potatoes are golden brown.

4. Top with Mushroom Gravy (see recipe, page 19).

BUTTERNUT
MAC & CHEESE

YIELD: 6-8 SERVINGS | COOK TIME: 30 MINUTES

INGREDIENTS:

1-2 BOXES WHOLE WHEAT MACARONI
NOODLES OR OTHER PASTA OF CHOICE

2 TBSP. SHALLOTS, PEELED AND CHOPPED

2-3 MEDIUM YUKON GOLD POTATOES, PEELED
AND CHOPPED

2 MEDIUM CARROTS, PEELED AND CHOPPED

½ ONION, PEELED AND CHOPPED

¼ BUTTERNUT SQUASH, PEELED AND CHOPPED

1 CUP WATER OR LOW-SODIUM
VEGETABLE BROTH

1 CUP RAW UNSALTED CASHEWS

3 GARLIC CLOVES

1 TBSP. DIJON MUSTARD

1 TBSP. LIQUID AMINOS

1 LEMON, JUICED

1 TSP. BLACK PEPPER

½ CUP NUTRITIONAL YEAST

½-1 CUP COOKING WATER

CAYENNE PEPPER & PAPRIKA FOR GARNISH

DIRECTIONS:

1. Boil butternut squash, carrots, shallots, onions and potatoes in a large pot.

2. In a separate pot, cook pasta according to package instructions.. Drain and
   set aside.

3. While veggies and pasta are cooking, put all remaining ingredients in a high speed
   blender and blend until smooth to make a cashew cheese base. If needed, add a
   small amount of the hot cooking water from the vegetables to the blender to make
   cashew cheese smooth (try to keep sauce thick though).

4. Once veggies have cooked soft, add them to the blender on top of the cashew
   cheese and blend until no lumps remain. You might need to do this in batches if
   the vegetables don't all fit into the blender (you can also use an immersion blender
   if preferred)

5. Taste cheese sauce and adjust seasoning according to preference.

6. Pour cheese sauce over cooked pasta and mix until cheese sauce coats all of the
   noodles evenly. Top with cayenne or paprika.

SOUTHERN
BBQ BOWL

YIELD: 3-4 BOWLS | COOK TIME: 45 MINUTES

INGREDIENTS:

CORNBREAD

2 CUPS CORNMEAL

1 CUP WHOLE WHEAT FLOUR

2 TSP. BAKING POWDER

2 CUPS UNSWEETENED SOY MILK

1 TBSP. APPLE CIDER VINEGAR

2 TBSP. MAPLE SYRUP

⅓ CUP APPLESAUCE

BOWL

2 BUNCHES COLLARD GREENS, DE-STEMMED AND SHREDDED

2 - 15OZ CANS BLACK-EYED PEAS, RINSED AND DRAINED

2-3 MEDIUM BEAUREGARD OR JEWEL SWEET POTATOES

2 - 8OZ PACKAGES TEMPEH, DICED INTO HALF-INCH CUBES

BBQ SAUCE (SEE RECIPE, PAGE 23)

HOT SAUCE OF CHOICE (OPTIONAL)

DIRECTIONS:

Cornbread

1. Preheat oven to 350 degrees Fahrenheit.

2. Add the soy milk and apple cider vinegar to a medium-sized mixing bowl and whisk until mixture starts to froth (about 1 minute). Set aside.

3. In a separate large mixing bowl, combine all dry cornbread ingredients.

4. Add maple syrup and applesauce to the soy milk mixture and stir well.

5. Pour wet ingredients into dry ingredient bowl and mix well.

6. Grease a 9" x 13" baking pan and pour in the batter so that it is distributed evenly.

7. Place pan in oven on center rack and bake for 30-35 minutes or until a golden brown crust forms on top.

Tempeh

1. Place chopped tempeh on a parchment-lined baking sheet and bake at 350 degrees Fahrenheit for 20-25 minutes (you can do this at the same time as the cornbread). Give the pan a shake about halfway through to move the tempeh around and prevent sticking.

2. Once cooked, toss tempeh in a desired amount of BBQ sauce.

Greens

1. Add about ½ inch water to a medium pot. Place on stove at medium-low heat and add the chopped greens.

2. Let greens steam for 15-20 minutes or until they are soft (but not soggy), stirring frequently.

Black-Eyed Peas

1. Add black-eyed peas to a large microwave safe bowl and cover with a paper towel. Microwave until hot (about 3-4 minutes), giving them a stir halfway through to make sure they are evenly heated.

Sweet Potatoes

1. Wash the potatoes and poke holes in them on all sides with a fork or knife. Wrap each one in a wet paper towel so that they are entirely covered. Microwave until tender (2-3 minutes for smaller potatoes, 3-4 minutes for larger potatoes).

2. Slice or dice the cooked potatoes however you like.

Bowl Assembly

1. Fill a large bowl with a desired amount of BBQ tempeh, collard greens, sweet potatoes, and black-eyed peas.

2. Drizzle with hot sauce or more BBQ sauce.

3. Top with a piece of cornbread.

MUSHROOM
TOFU TACOS

YIELD: 4-6 TACOS | COOK TIME: 30 MINUTES

INGREDIENTS:

TACOS

1 BLOCK TOFU, DRAINED & PRESSED

½ ONION, DICED

½ GREEN BELL PEPPER, DICED

1 CAN BLACK BEANS, DRAINED & RINSED

1 CAN PINTO BEANS, DRAINED & RINSED

2 ROMA TOMATOES, DICED

1 PACK HARD TACO SHELLS (OR USE TORTILLAS
FOR SOFT TACOS)

LETTUCE OF CHOICE

CASHEW CHEESE TO TASTE
(SEE RECIPE, PAGE 14)

HOT SAUCE OF CHOICE

SALSA

TACO SEASONING

½ TBSP. CUMIN

½ TBSP. CHILI POWDER

½ TBSP. OREGANO

½ TBSP. PAPRIKA

½ TBSP. ONION POWDER

½ TBSP. GARLIC POWDER

½ TBSP. BLACK PEPPER

½ TBSP. SMOKED PAPRIKA

½ TBSP. BASIL

DIRECTIONS:

1. Preheat oven to 425 degrees Fahrenheit. Spread crumbled tofu out on a baking sheet.

2. Mix all taco seasoning spices together in a small bowl and pour over tofu. Add diced onion and bell pepper on top, then mix well. Bake in the oven for 15 minutes.

3. Remove tofu and veggies from oven and add black beans, pinto beans, and tomatoes. Mix and bake for another 8-10 minutes.

4. Once tofu/bean/veggie mixture is done, remove from oven. Assemble tacos by stuffing shell with tofu mixture and topping with lettuce, cashew cheese and hot sauce or salsa to taste.

5. Tip: You can make a large batch of taco seasoning and store it in a mason jar so you have taco seasoning ready to go any time!

BLACK BEAN
BURGERS

YIELD: 12 BURGER PATTIES | COOK TIME: 35 MINUTES

INGREDIENTS:

BURGERS

1 CAN BLACK BEANS, DRAINED AND RINSED

2 CUPS ROLLED OATS

1 CUP BREADCRUMBS

1 CUP SPINACH OR KALE

2 CARROTS, CHOPPED

1 ONION, CHOPPED

1 CUP MUSHROOMS, CHOPPED

1 TBSP. KETCHUP

1 TBSP. YELLOW MUSTARD OR SPICY
BROWN MUSTARD

2 TBSP. CUMIN

2 TBSP. CHILI POWDER

1 TBSP. OREGANO

1 TBSP. NUTRITIONAL YEAST

2 TSP. BLACK PEPPER

WHOLE WHEAT HAMBURGER BUNS
FOR SERVING

OPTIONAL TOPPINGS FOR SERVING:

ROMAINE LETTUCE

TOMATOES

SLICED ONIONS

KETCHUP

MUSTARD

DIRECTIONS:

1. Preheat oven to 425 degrees Fahrenheit.

2. Add all burger ingredients except oats and breadcrumbs to a food processor or high-speed blender.

3. Process until well combined. If it's still a little chunky, that's okay!

4. Transfer mixture from food processor to a bowl. Stir in oats and breadcrumbs, slowly adding more until the mixture becomes thick and dry enough that you can form patties with your hands.

5. Form 3"-wide patties with hands and place on a parchment-lined baking sheet. Continue forming patties until you have used all of the burger mixture in the bowl.

6. Bake in the oven for 10 minutes. Remove pan from oven, flip burgers, and cook for 15 additional minutes. Burgers are done when a slightly golden brown crust forms on each side.

7. Serve on buns with whatever combination of optional toppings you like!

LASAGNA

YIELD: 8-12 SERVINGS | COOK TIME: 50 MINUTES

INGREDIENTS:

15 WHOLE WHEAT LASAGNA NOODLES
5 CUPS NATURAL MARINARA SAUCE
1 ZUCCHINI, DICED
4 OZ (HALF AN 8OZ PACKAGE) WHITE BUTTON OR CREMINI MUSHROOMS, DE-STEMMED AND CHOPPED
½ SMALL YELLOW OR WHITE ONION, CHOPPED
2 GARLIC CLOVES, MINCED
1 CUP FROZEN PEAS

1 CUP FROZEN CHOPPED SPINACH
2 - 14OZ PACKAGES EXTRA FIRM TOFU, DRAINED AND PRESSED
1 - 8OZ PACKAGE PLAIN HUMMUS (LOOK FOR AN OIL-FREE VARIETY!)
½ CUP NUTRITIONAL YEAST
¼ CUP FRESH BASIL, FINELY CHOPPED
1 TSP. GARLIC POWDER

DIRECTIONS:

1. Preheat oven to 350 degrees Fahrenheit.

2. In a medium skillet over medium-high heat, add the zucchini, mushrooms, garlic, onion, and a splash of water or vegetable broth. Sauté for five minutes. Add the frozen peas and spinach and cook for an additional five minutes, stirring frequently.

3. While the veggies are cooking, use your hands to crumble the tofu blocks into a medium mixing bowl. Add the hummus, nutritional yeast, fresh basil, and garlic powder to the bowl. Stir until everything is evenly mixed.

4. Spread one cup of marinara sauce evenly over the bottom of a 9" x 13" baking pan. Cover the bottom of the pan with a partially overlapping layer of noodles (about five)

5. Layer half of the tofu ricotta mix over the noodles along with half of the sautéed veggies and one cup of the marinara sauce. Spread all ingredients evenly across the pan.

6. Repeat with another layer of noodles and the rest of the ricotta mixture, sautéed veggies, and another cup of marinara sauce. Cover with the last layer of noodles and the last 2 cups of marinara sauce.

7. Cover with foil and bake for 25 minutes. Remove foil, return to oven, and cook for an additional 10 minutes until all noodles are soft and the sauce begins to coagulate on top.

CHICKPEA BASIL
PIZZA

YIELD: 4 SERVINGS | COOK TIME: 30 MINUTES

INGREDIENTS:

1 WHOLE WHEAT PITA BREAD, LAVASH BREAD, OR PIZZA CRUST (YOU CAN BUY PIZZA DOUGH OR
MAKE YOUR OWN CRUST—UP TO YOU!)
2 CANS CHICKPEAS (GARBANZO BEANS)
1 CUP SPINACH
1 RED ONION, SLICED THIN
1 TBSP. MINCED GARLIC
2 TSP. OLIVE OIL
2 TSP. RED PEPPER FLAKES

BASIL PESTO SAUCE:
1 CUP CASHEWS
1 CUP BASIL
½ CUP PINE NUTS
1 LEMON, JUICED
1 TBSP. DIJON MUSTARD
1 TBSP. LIQUID AMINOS
1 TBSP. GARLIC SALT
1 TBSP. BLACK PEPPERWATER TO THIN SAUCE AND MAKE SMOOTHER

DIRECTIONS:

1. Preheat oven to 400 degrees Fahrenheit.

2. Sauté chickpeas with garlic and vegetable broth in a medium pan over medium
    heat. After about 2 minutes, add red onions and cook for 3-5 additional minutes.
    Set aside.

3. Prepare basil pesto sauce by combining all sauce ingredients in a blender and
    blending until smooth.

4. Spread pesto sauce over crust.

5. Top with desired amount of chickpeas, onions, spinach, and red pepper flakes.

6. Bake for 10-15 minutes or until crust is crispy.

BBQ JACKFRUIT
SLIDERS

YIELD: 8-10 SLIDERS | COOK TIME: 25 MINUTES

INGREDIENTS:

2 CANS YOUNG JACKFRUIT IN *BRINE* (NOT SYRUP)

2 TBSP. LOW-SODIUM VEGETABLE BROTH (FOR SAUTÉING)

1 ONION, DICED

1 TBSP. LIQUID SMOKE

½ TBSP. LIQUID AMINOS OR COCONUT AMINOS

1 TBSP. GARLIC, MINCED

1 TSP. CHILI POWDER

1 TBSP. PAPRIKA

2 TSP. SMOKED PAPRIKA

2 TSP. CUMIN

BLACK PEPPER TO TASTE

BBQ SAUCE TO TASTE (SEE RECIPE, PAGE 23)

DIRECTIONS:

1. Drain and rinse jackfruit and remove from can. Cut out the hard core part from each piece and remove the big seeds (these don't get soft very easily, so we only want the easily shreddable pieces). Shred remaining soft parts into small pieces with fingers and place in a medium sized bowl.

2. Sauté onion and garlic with 2 tbsp. vegetable broth in the bottom of a medium pot until the onion becomes translucent.

3. While onion and garlic are cooking, cover jackfruit with liquid smoke, liquid aminos, chili powder, paprika, smoked paprika, cumin, and black pepper.

4. Once onions are translucent, add jackfruit to the pan with the onions and garlic. Cook until lightly golden brown.

5. Top jackfruit with BBQ sauce.

6. Serve on slider buns with slaw or raw purple cabbage.

Tip: You can also cook this in a Crock-Pot or slow cooker. To do so, simply dump the entire can of drained jackfruit in with the spices and BBQ sauce and cook on low for 8 hours. There's no need to separate out the jackfruit parts with this method, because we'll be cooking for long enough that everything will soften up.

P O K E
BOWL

YIELD: 4-5 SERVINGS | COOK TIME: 50 MINUTES

INGREDIENTS:

PINEAPPLE RICE:
2 CUPS UNCOOKED BROWN RICE
½ CUP PINEAPPLE JUICE
1 TBSP. RICE VINEGAR

MUSHROOMS:
2 CUPS SHIITAKE MUSHROOMS, DE-STEMMED AND SLICED
1 TBSP. SOY SAUCE
2 TBSP. LOW-SODIUM VEGETABLE BROTH OR WATER

SESAME VEGGIES:
1 MEDIUM CARROT, CUT LENGTHWISE AND SLICED INTO THIN HALF MOONS
1 MEDIUM RADISH, CUT LENGTHWISE AND SLICED INTO THIN HALF MOONS
½ OF A MEDIUM CUCUMBER OR ZUCCHINI, CUT LENGTHWISE AND SLICED INTO THIN HALF MOONS
2 TSP. SESAME OIL

OTHER FRUITS AND VEGGIES:
1 - 16OZ BAG FROZEN SHELLED EDAMAME
1 CUP SHREDDED OR CHOPPED RED CABBAGE
1 BELL PEPPER (YELLOW, RED, OR ORANGE), JULIENNE CUT
¾ CUP DICED MANGO (YOU CAN USE FRESH MANGO OR THAWED FROZEN MANGO)
1 AVOCADO, SLICED

OPTIONAL TOPPINGS:
PICKLED GINGER
PICKLED RED ONION
SOY SAUCE
SRIRACHA
PANDA SEEDS (A MIX OF BLACK AND WHITE SESAME SEEDS)
NORI SHEETS
WASABI PEAS (OPTIONAL)

DIRECTIONS:

1. Cook rice in a rice cooker or on the stove top. Mix with pineapple juice and rice vinegar. Set aside.

2. While the rice is cooking, sauté the mushrooms over medium heat using vegetable broth (or water) and soy sauce. Stir frequently. Cook until mushrooms are tender and liquid has evaporated (about 8-10 minutes). Remove from heat and set aside.

3. Prepare the sesame veggies by tossing the sliced carrot, radish, and cucumber with sesame oil. Set aside.

4. Pour the frozen edamame in a large microwave-safe bowl and cover with a paper towel. Microwave for 2 minutes, give it a stir, and then microwave for another 1-2 minutes or until heated evenly. Set aside.

5. Prepare the red cabbage, bell pepper, mango, and avocado. Set aside.

6. Prepare any of the desired optional toppings and set aside.

7. Once everything is cooked and prepared, assemble bowls by starting with a bed of rice and piling on the veggie sides, condiments, and toppings. Enjoy!

STUFFED ACORN
SQUASH

YIELD: 4 SERVINGS | COOK TIME: 70 MINUTES

INGREDIENTS:

2 ACORN SQUASH, CUT IN HALF AND SEEDED

1 CUP DRY WILD RICE

2 CUPS LOW-SODIUM VEGETABLE BROTH, PLUS
MORE TO SAUTÉ VEGGIES

2 GARLIC CLOVES, MINCED

½ SMALL/MEDIUM YELLOW ONION,
FINELY CHOPPED

3 CELERY RIBS, FINELY CHOPPED

1 MEDIUM CARROT, FINELY CHOPPED

1 CUP WHITE BUTTON MUSHROOMS,
FINELY CHOPPED

1 - 15OZ CAN OF LENTILS, DRAINED
AND RINSED

1 TSP. DRIED THYME

½ TSP. DRIED GROUND SAGE

½ TSP. DRIED ROSEMARY

¼ TSP. BLACK PEPPER

⅓ CUP CHOPPED RAW PECANS

½ CUP DRIED CRANBERRIES

DIRECTIONS:

1. Preheat oven to 375 degrees Fahrenheit.

2. Place the squash flesh side down on a parchment-lined baking sheet. Bake for
   45 minutes.

3. While squash is cooking, add the wild rice and two cups of vegetable broth to a
   small pot. Bring to a boil, then reduce heat to low and simmer for 30-40 minutes.
   Drain off any excess fluid and set aside.

4. While the squash and rice are cooking, add the garlic, onion, celery, carrot,
   mushrooms, and a splash of vegetable broth to a large skillet. Sauté over medium-
   high heat until tender (about 12-15 minutes). Once the veggies are cooked, add the
   thyme, sage, rosemary, and black pepper and cook for an additional minute, stirring
   well. Remove from heat.

5. In a large bowl, combine the sautéed vegetables, lentils, pecans, dried cranberries,
   and cooked rice. Mix well.

6. When the squash halves have cooked, remove them from the oven and scoop
   an even amount of the filling mixture into each one (don't be afraid to load them
   up). Place the filled squash halves back in the oven flesh side up and cook for an
   additional 10 minutes (you may need to adjust the rack height in your oven). If there
   is any extra filling, feel free to eat as is, or use it to refill the squash after some has
   been eaten.

7. After 10 minutes, remove squash from the oven and serve immediately.

CHICKPEA "TUNA"
NOODLE CASSEROLE

YIELD: 4-6 SERVINGS | COOK TIME: 65 MINUTES

INGREDIENTS:

1 BOX PASTA OF CHOICE

FILLING:

2 CANS CHICKPEAS, DRAINED & RINSED
1 CUP PORTABELLA MUSHROOMS, CHOPPED
2 CUPS SHIITAKE MUSHROOMS, CHOPPED
1 YELLOW ONION, DICED
½ CUP PEAS, FRESH OR FROZEN
½ CUP CORN, FRESH OR FROZEN
BLACK PEPPER TO TASTE

SAUCE:

1 CUP VEGETABLE BROTH
½ CUP UNSWEETENED NON-DAIRY MILK
½ CUP NUTRITIONAL YEAST
2 TBSP. LIQUID AMINOS
1 TBSP. THYME
½ TBSP. ROSEMARY
1 TBSP. GARLIC POWDER
1 TBSP. ONION POWDER
1 TSP. BLACK PEPPER

DIRECTIONS:

1. Cook pasta according to package instructions. Drain and rinse with cold water. Set aside.

2. In a food processor, pulse chickpeas just until coarsely chopped--be sure not to go too far and purée them.

3. In a large sauté pan, add a splash of vegetable broth and diced onion. Sauté until onions are soft and translucent. Set one-half of the onions aside. Add the mushrooms to the remaining onions and continue to sauté until onions are caramelized.

4. In a small saucepan, combine all of the sauce ingredients and whisk until smooth. Add a small amount of flour if you would like the mixture to be thicker (it will thicken slightly as it cooks and cools)

5. Add the sauce, onions you set aside, chickpeas, peas, and corn to the mushroom mixture in the large pan.

6. Add the cooked pasta to the pan and mix well. Pour into a glass 9" x 13" baking dish. Bake for 30-35 minutes until slightly golden and cooked through.

7. Garnish with parsley and serve with a crusty loaf of bread or veggies of your choice.

PURA VIDA
BOWL

YIELD: 3-4 SERVINGS | COOK TIME: 45 MINUTES

INGREDIENTS:

1 ½ CUPS UNCOOKED BROWN RICE

2 - 15OZ CANS BLACK BEANS, DRAINED AND RINSED

1 BUNCH OF KALE, DE-STEMMED AND TORN INTO CHIP-SIZED PIECES

2 MEDIUM SWEET POTATOES, DICED

1 CUP RED CABBAGE, SHREDDED

1 - 15OZ CAN OF CORN, DRAINED AND RINSED

RECOMMENDED TOPPINGS:

½ RED ONION

¼ CUP CILANTRO

½ LIME

SALSA TO TASTE

HOT SAUCE TO TASTE

DIRECTIONS:

1. Cook the brown rice in a rice cooker or on the stovetop.

2. Preheat oven to 400 degrees Fahrenheit. Spread diced sweet potato on a parchment-lined baking sheet and bake for 30-40 minutes or until potatoes are tender and golden brown.

3. Add kale to a small pot or skillet. Cover the bottom of the pot with a thin layer of water and cook on medium-low until the kale has softened. Remove from heat.

4. Warm black beans in the microwave.

5. Once the brown rice, sweet potatoes, and kale are cooked, assemble by adding portions of each ingredient to a small section of the bowl. Top with cilantro, diced red onion, lime juice, salsa, and hot sauce.

DIET AND CARDIOVASCULAR HEALTH

COLE ADAM, RD

Cardiovascular disease (CVD), which includes heart attacks, heart failure, and strokes, is the leading cause of death in the United States and worldwide. However, an estimated 90% of deaths from CVD could be prevented with a healthy diet and lifestyle.[19] Maintaining a healthy body weight, not smoking, getting regular exercise, and managing stress are all ways to lower CVD risk.

The best diet for cardiovascular health is a whole food, plant-based diet low in added fats. This diet is not only associated with the lowest rates of CVD, but it is also the only diet proven to *reverse* coronary artery disease.[1,20] It allows the body to remove plaque from plaque-laden arteries, improving blood flow to the heart and throughout the body.

Leone/Pixabay

A whole food, plant-based diet omits foods known to be detrimental to cardiovascular health and incorporates foods that are protective. Meat, high-fat dairy, eggs, highly processed foods, added oil, added salt, added sugar, and other junk foods are known to be detrimental to our cardiovascular system. These foods cause inflammation, impair blood flow, and increase blood pressure and blood cholesterol levels, so their consumption is associated with an increased risk of developing CVD.[21,22] On the flip side, beans, whole grains, fruits, vegetables, nuts, and seeds all promote good cardiovascular health. These foods are rich in fiber, potassium, magnesium, plant-based protein, healthy fat, and thousands of phytochemicals that reduce inflammation, enhance blood flow, and keep our blood vessels nice and clean.[20]

Most whole plant-based foods are great for cardiovascular health, but there are a few foods that appear especially heart-healthy:

Beans are packed with nutrients that are essential for good cardiovascular function, such as potassium and magnesium. They are also high in fiber, which can help lower cholesterol and stabilize blood sugar levels.

Dark leafy green vegetables such as kale, spinach, collards, and arugula are a good source of potassium, magnesium, and fiber as well. They also contain plant-based nitrates, which work in a manner similar to the prescription nitrates people take for chest pain. When we eat dark leafy greens, our body converts these nitrates into nitric oxide, which is a gas released by the cells lining our blood vessels. Nitric oxide helps our blood vessels dilate, which keeps blood flowing smoothly through them and prevents plaque buildup.

Berries are packed with antioxidants and nutrients that reduce inflammation. Some of these nutrients include the pigments responsible for the deep blue, black, and red color of most berries. Regular berry consumption has been shown to lower blood pressure, lower cholesterol levels, and reduce inflammation, making them an extremely heart-healthy food.[23,24]

For ideal cardiovascular health, we should consume a whole food, plant-based diet centered on whole grains, beans, fruits, and vegetables. We should also make an extra effort to include beans, dark leafy greens, and berries into our diet, as these foods appear extremely effective at improving cardiovascular health. Combine this diet pattern with other healthy lifestyle behaviors and our hearts will keep ticking long into old age.

DIET AND BRAIN HEALTH

COLE ADAM, RD

It was once thought that being diagnosed with dementia (such as Alzheimer's disease and other illnesses) was the result of bad luck or bad genetics. And while it's true that our genes play a role when it comes to brain health, it is now well-established that our lifestyle—how often we exercise, whether or not we smoke tobacco, how we manage stress, how much sleep we get, and what we eat—plays a much larger role than our genetics. This is good news. It means we have more control over our long-term health than we once thought.

A healthy lifestyle is essential for warding off dementia and other forms of cognitive decline. When it comes to diet, certain foods are consistently associated with an increased risk of dementia. These foods include meat, high-fat dairy, fried foods, and sweets. On the other hand, a plant-based, Mediterranean-style diet has been found to be extremely protective.[25,26,27] This means we should eat a diet rich in fruits, vegetables, whole grains, legumes (beans, lentils, split peas), nuts, and seeds. The more we consume these foods, the more we lower our risk of developing dementia.

In addition to a whole food plant-based diet, there are certain foods that appear especially protective against Alzheimer's and other forms of dementia. These include foods rich in flavonoids, dark leafy greens, and moderate amounts of plant-based fats.

Flavonoids are compounds found in a variety of plants. They appear to have numerous health-promoting properties, especially when it comes to brain health. Foods rich in flavonoids include citrus fruits, black and green tea, herbs such as parsley and thyme, soybeans, red grapes, plums, apples, cocoa, and berries. In fact, berries may be one of the best foods for our brain, as research suggests that regular berry consumption may slow the progression of cognitive decline.[28,29]

Dark leafy greens are among the healthiest foods we can consume, so it's no surprise that daily consumption of dark leafy greens is linked with improved memory and slower rates of cognitive decline. One study found that older adults eating a serving a day of dark leafy greens had a cognitive decline rate that was the equivalent of being 11 years younger in age, compared to age-matched individuals who didn't consume dark leafy greens.[30]

Fat is essential for optimal brain health. However, not all fats are created equal. Saturated and trans fats, predominantly found in animal products and processed foods, are detrimental to our brain and overall health. Conversely, the consumption of fat from whole, plant-based sources promotes overall health and optimal brain function. Good sources of plant-based fat include: avocado, olives, nuts, and seeds (especially walnuts, flaxseed, chia seeds, and hemp seeds). These foods can be consumed in small amounts daily.

How well our brain ages is largely within our control. The same lifestyle behaviors that lower our risk for cardiovascular disease, type 2 diabetes, cancer, and other chronic illnesses can also prevent or delay the onset of Alzheimer's disease and other forms of dementia. For optimal brain health, exercise regularly, avoid smoking tobacco, find ways to manage and lower stress, get adequate sleep, and consume a plant-based diet that emphasizes the foods recommended above.

soups

MINESTRONE
SOUP

YIELD: 4-6 SERVINGS | COOK TIME: 30 MINUTES OR 4-6 HOURS IF USING SLOW COOKER

INGREDIENTS:

1 ONION, DICED

2 CARROTS, DICED

2 CELERY STICKS, DICED

1 BOX PASTA, COOKED (MAKE SURE NOT TO COOK IT IN THE SOUP--COOK IT SEPARATELY!)

2 TOMATOES, DICED

2 TBSP. TOMATO PASTE

2 CUPS SPINACH OR KALE

¼ CUP NUTRITIONAL YEAST

3 CLOVES GARLIC, MINCED

2 TSP. OREGANO

1 TSP. SAGE

1 TSP. THYME

2 TSP. BLACK PEPPER

2 TSP. GARLIC SALT

½ TSP. CAYENNE PEPPER

1 TSP. SMOKED PAPRIKA

2 BAY LEAVES

1 - 15OZ CAN KIDNEY BEANS

1 - 15OZ CAN WHITE BEANS

1 ZUCCHINI

6 CUPS LOW-SODIUM VEGETABLE BROTH

DIRECTIONS:

If making soup in a Crock-Pot (slow cooker):

1. Place everything in the crock pot EXCEPT the pasta and cook on high for 4-6 hours, stirring every 2 hours. Stir in pasta during the last 15 minutes of cooking.

2. Season as desired.

If not cooking in a slow cooker:

1. In the bottom of a large soup pot, sauté the carrots, onion, garlic and celery in a splash of vegetable broth.

2. Add in zucchini and tomatoes. Cook for 5 more minutes until all veggies are soft.

3. Add in all spices and tomato paste and stir well.

4. Stir in the rest of the vegetable broth and the beans. Simmer for 5 minutes.

5. Add in pasta and spinach.

6. Taste and adjust seasoning as needed.

BUTTERNUT SQUASH &
APPLE SOUP

YIELD: 4-6 SERVINGS | COOK TIME: 25 MINUTES

INGREDIENTS:

1 BUTTERNUT SQUASH, DICED

2 APPLES, DICED

1 YELLOW ONION, DICED

2 CARROTS, DICED

2 TBSP. FRESH GINGER, MINCED

5 CUPS LOW-SODIUM VEGETABLE BROTH

½ LEMON, JUICED

1 TBSP. HEMP SEEDS (OPTIONAL)

2 TSP. THYME

2 TSP. GARLIC SALT

2 TBSP. NUTRITIONAL YEAST (OPTIONAL)

2 TSP. BLACK PEPPER

1 TSP. CINNAMON

1 TSP. TURMERIC

3 CLOVES GARLIC, MINCED

½ CUP UNSWEETENED PLAIN ALMOND MILK (OR ANY NON-DAIRY MILK OF CHOICE)

DIRECTIONS:

1. Sauté garlic, carrots, and onions with 4 tbsp. vegetable broth in the bottom of a large soup pot over medium heat.

2. Once onions become translucent, add in apples and squash.

3. Add the rest of the vegetable broth to the pot and simmer until squash is soft.

4. Once squash is soft, add in all spices and simmer for another 5 minutes.

5. Remove soup from heat and stir in almond milk and lemon juice.

6. You can leave this soup chunky or puree it in a blender or with an immersion blender. If blending, blend after adding the almond milk and lemon juice. (We like it best blended!)

7. Adjust seasoning to taste and serve warm. Garnish with diced apples and hemp seeds.

30 MINUTE
CHILI

YIELD: 6-8 SERVINGS | COOK TIME: 30 MINUTES

INGREDIENTS:

3 GARLIC CLOVES, MINCED

½ YELLOW OR WHITE ONION, DICED

2 CARROTS, DICED INTO PEA-SIZED PIECES

3 CELERY RIBS, CHOPPED

½ GREEN OR RED BELL PEPPER, DICED INTO PEA-SIZED PIECES

¼ CUP LOW-SODIUM VEGETABLE BROTH OR WATER

1 CUP CHOPPED FROZEN SPINACH

3 - 15OZ CANS DIFFERENT TYPES OF BEANS, DRAINED AND RINSED (WE USE BLACK BEANS,
NAVY BEANS, AND KIDNEY BEANS, BUT PICK WHAT YOU LIKE BEST!)

1 - 15OZ CAN DICED TOMATOES

1 - 15OZ CAN TOMATO SAUCE

32OZ TOMATO JUICE

1 TSP. DRIED OREGANO

1 TSP. GROUND CUMIN

½ TSP. BLACK PEPPER (MORE TO TASTE)

¼ TSP. CAYENNE PEPPER (MORE TO TASTE)

¼ CUP CHILI POWDER (MORE TO TASTE)

DIRECTIONS:

1. Add garlic, onions, carrots, celery, bell pepper, and vegetable broth to the bottom of a large soup pot. Sauté over medium-high heat for 10 minutes or until veggies are tender.

2. Add the frozen spinach and sauté for 5 more minutes.

3. Add all remaining ingredients (including liquid ingredients) to the pot and stir well.

4. Bring chili to a boil, stirring frequently. Reduce heat to low and simmer for at least 10 minutes.

5. Remove from heat and serve with whole grain bread or crackers.

CHICKPEA
NOODLE SOUP

YIELD: 4-6 SERVINGS | COOK TIME: 20 MINUTES

INGREDIENTS:

1 BOX PASTA OF CHOICE, COOKED AL DENTE (MAKE SURE TO COOK SEPARATELY FROM SOUP!)

2 CANS CHICKPEAS, DRAINED & RINSED

6 CUPS VEGETABLE BROTH

4 LARGE CARROTS, DICED

1 YELLOW ONION, DICED

4 CELERY STALKS, DICED

3 GARLIC CLOVES, MINCED

1 TBSP. FRESH THYME

1 TBSP. DRIED ROSEMARY

1 TBSP. DRIED OREGANO

3 TBSP. NUTRITIONAL YEAST

2 TSP. BLACK PEPPER

1 TSP. CHILI FLAKES (OPTIONAL)

DIRECTIONS:

1. Heat 2 tbsp. vegetable broth in the bottom of a large saucepan. Add in carrots, onion, celery and garlic. Cook until onions are translucent, about 8 minutes.

2. Once veggies are soft, stir in all of the spices and the rest of the vegetable broth.

3. Simmer for 10 minutes on low heat, then add in chickpeas and cooked pasta.

4. Cook on low heat for 5 additional minutes.

5. Adjust seasonings if needed. Garnish with fresh thyme.

LENTIL
SOUP

YIELD: 4-6 SERVINGS | COOK TIME: 30 MINUTES

INGREDIENTS:

1 MEDIUM YELLOW OR WHITE ONION, CHOPPED

2 CARROTS, PEELED AND CHOPPED

1 ZUCCHINI, DICED

1 YELLOW SQUASH, DICED

4 GARLIC CLOVES, MINCED

2 TSP. GROUND CUMIN

1 TSP. CURRY POWDER

1 TSP. DRIED THYME

1 - 28OZ CAN DICED TOMATOES, DRAINED

1 CUP BROWN OR GREEN LENTILS, UNCOOKED

2-3 CUPS LOW-SODIUM VEGETABLE BROTH

2 CUPS WATER

1 TSP. BLACK PEPPER

1 CUP CHOPPED FRESH KALE

JUICE OF ½ TO 1 MEDIUM LEMON, TO TASTE

DIRECTIONS:

1. Add chopped onions and carrots to the bottom of a large soup pot with ¼ cup vegetable broth. Cook over medium heat until onions have softened and turned translucent, about 5 minutes.

2. Add the zucchini, squash, garlic, cumin, curry powder and thyme. Stir constantly until fragrant, about 30 seconds.

3. Pour in the diced tomatoes and cook for about 5 more minutes, stirring often in order to enhance flavor.

4. Add the lentils, black pepper, water, and the rest of the vegetable broth. Increase heat to medium-high and bring the soup to a boil, then partially cover the pot with a tilted lid, reduce heat, and simmer.

5. Cook for 30 minutes or until lentils are soft.

6. Remove 2 cups of soup from the pot and pour them into a blender. Purée until no lumps remain. Return the puréed soup to the pot and add the chopped kale.

7. Cook kale until kale wilts and softens.

8. Remove from heat and stir in the juice of ½ of a lemon. Taste and season with more pepper and/or lemon juice until the flavor is to your liking.

BAKED POTATO SOUP WITH
COCONUT "BACON"

YIELD: 4-6 SERVINGS | COOK TIME: 35 MINUTES

INGREDIENTS:

3 LARGE POTATOES, PEELED & DICED
½ HEAD CAULIFLOWER, CHOPPED
½ BUNDLE SCALLIONS, DICED + MORE FOR GARNISH
1 TBSP. GARLIC, MINCED
2 CELERY STALKS, DICED
½ YELLOW ONION, DICED
¼ CUP NUTRITIONAL YEAST
1 TBSP. WHITE VINEGAR
1 CUP RAW CASHEWS
1 TSP. BLACK PEPPER
1 TSP. PAPRIKA
1 TSP. SMOKED PAPRIKA
1-2 TSP. CHIPOTLE POWDER
1 TBSP. LIQUID AMINOS
½ CUP UNSWEETENED ALMOND MILK
1-3 CUPS LOW-SODIUM VEGETABLE BROTH

COCONUT BACON:

1 ½ CUPS LARGE UNSWEETENED COCONUT FLAKES
2 TSP. LIQUID SMOKE
2 TBSP. COCONUT AMINOS
1 TBSP. LIQUID AMINOS
2 TSP. SMOKED PAPRIKA
1 TSP. PAPRIKA
1 TSP. BLACK PEPPER
1 TBSP. MAPLE SYRUP

DIRECTIONS:

1. Preheat oven to 425 degrees Fahrenheit.

2. Spread potatoes and cauliflower out on a parchment-lined baking sheet. Cover with a splash of veggie broth. Bake for 10-15 minutes or until potatoes are soft.

3. While potatoes and cauliflower are cooking, prepare coconut bacon by placing all coconut bacon ingredients except coconut flakes in a bowl. Mix well, then pour in coconut flakes and mix until flakes are evenly coated.

4. Pour coconut onto a baking sheet, making sure to spread it out evenly. Bake at 425 degrees Fahrenheit for 10 minutes or until coconut bacon is crispy.

5. Sauté the white ends of the scallions with garlic, onions, and celery in a splash of vegetable broth. Once veggies are soft, add paprika, smoked paprika, chipotle powder, nutritional yeast, raw cashews, liquid aminos, and vinegar. Cook for 5-10 minutes, stirring often.

6. Pour the veggie/cashew mixture into a high speed blender.

7. Add the cooked potatoes and cauliflower to the blender along with almond milk and 1 cup of vegetable broth. Blend until creamy, stopping to check the thickness every few minutes. If the soup is too thick, add more liquid. Continue blending and adding liquid until the soup is smooth and there are no solid chunks remaining.

8. Top with coconut bacon and the green ends of the scallions. Serve warm with a side of toasted bread.

BROCCOLI
CHEESE SOUP

YIELD: 4-6 SERVINGS | COOK TIME: 40 MINUTES

INGREDIENTS:

4 LARGE YUKON GOLD POTATOES, CHOPPED

4 CUPS LOW-SODIUM VEGETABLE BROTH

2 MEDIUM CARROTS, CHOPPED

1 HEAD BROCCOLI, CHOPPED

1 WHITE OR YELLOW ONION, CHOPPED

¾ CUPS ALMOND MILK OR OTHER PLANT-BASED MILK

WATER TO BOIL

WHITE BEAN CHEESE:

1 CAN WHITE BEANS, DRAINED & RINSED
(SUB CASHEWS FOR A CREAMIER VERSION, IF DESIRED)

½ CUP NUTRITIONAL YEAST

2 GARLIC CLOVES, MINCED

½ LEMON, JUICED

1 TBSP. LIQUID AMINOS

½ CUP VEGETABLE BROTH OR WATER

1 TBSP. DIJON MUSTARD

2 TSP. PAPRIKA

1 TSP. THYME

1 TSP. OREGANO

BLACK PEPPER TO TASTE

DIRECTIONS:

1. Boil potatoes, onions, carrots, and broccoli in water until soft. Strain or remove from water (be sure to save about a cup of your cooking water)

2. Make White Bean Cheese by adding all White Bean Cheese ingredients to a high speed blender and blending until completely smooth. Transfer to a separate container and set aside.

3. One veggies are soft, transfer them to the blender and blend until smooth (it's okay if a few small chunks remain).

4. Combine blended white bean cheese and blended vegetables in a large pot.

5. Stir in almond milk and some of the cooking water you saved from earlier.

6. Blend soup either with an immersion blender or by transferring it to a high speed blender in batches and blending one batch at a time.

7. If using a high speed blender, transfer the blended soup back to the pot.

8. Simmer on low heat for 10-20 minutes, adjusting seasonings as desired.

9. Serve with warm toasted bread.

PORTOBELLO
POT ROAST

YIELD: 4-5 SERVINGS | COOK TIME: 35 MINUTES

INGREDIENTS:

5 LARGE YUKON GOLD POTATOES, DICED INTO 1-INCH CUBES
3 CARROTS, SLICED INTO COINS
1 ONION, DICED
4 LARGE PORTOBELLO MUSHROOMS, CUT INTO 1-INCH SLICES
3 GARLIC CLOVES, MINCED
3 CUPS LOW-SODIUM VEGETABLE BROTH
½ TBSP. LIQUID AMINOS
1 TBSP. ANNIE'S ORGANIC VEGAN WORCESTERSHIRE SAUCE
2 TBSP. RED WINE VINEGAR
1 TBSP. DRIED BASIL
1 TBSP. DRIED ROSEMARY
1 TBSP. DRIED THYME
1 TBSP. DRIED SAGE
2 TSP. BLACK PEPPER

DIRECTIONS:

1. Sauté onions and garlic with 4 tbsp. vegetable broth in the bottom of a large pot.

2. Once onions are soft and translucent, add in mushrooms, red wine vinegar, and all spices. Cook until mushrooms are soft.

3. Once mushrooms are soft, add in carrots, potatoes and the remaining vegetable broth.

4. Simmer 20-25 minutes or until veggies are soft.

5. Stir in worcestershire sauce and liquid aminos. Taste and adjust seasoning if needed. Simmer for 5-10 more minutes and serve warm.

AFRICAN
PEANUT SOUP

YIELD: 6-8 | COOK TIME: 45 MINUTES

INGREDIENTS:

1 RED ONION, CHOPPED

4 GARLIC CLOVES, MINCED

2 TBSP. FRESH GINGER, MINCED OR GRATED

7 CUPS LOW-SODIUM VEGETABLE BROTH

2 MEDIUM CARROTS, QUARTERED LENGTHWISE
THEN CUT INTO ½ INCH CHUNKS

2 CUPS BUTTERNUT SQUASH (ABOUT ONE
SMALL SQUASH), PEELED, SEEDED, AND CUT
INTO ½ INCH CUBES

1 CUP DRIED RED LENTILS, RINSED
AND DRAINED

1 BUNCH COLLARD GREENS, WASHED,
DE-STEMMED, FINELY CHOPPED

¾ CUP TOMATO PASTE

½ CUP NATURAL PEANUT BUTTER (SMOOTH
OR CHUNKY)

2 TBSP. SRIRACHA OR OTHER HOT CHILI SAUCE

1 TSP. GROUND TURMERIC

1 - 15OZ CAN CHICKPEAS (GARBANZO BEANS),
DRAINED AND RINSED

½ TSP. BLACK PEPPER, OR MORE TO TASTE

OPTIONAL GARNISHES:
CILANTRO

PEANUTS

EXTRA HOT SAUCE OR SRIRACHA

DIRECTIONS:

1. Add garlic, ginger, onion, and ½ cup of vegetable broth to a large pot. Cook for 3-4 minutes over medium-low heat, stirring frequently.

2. Add the carrots, squash, and collard greens to the pot. Cook for 5 more minutes, stirring frequently.

3. Add remaining broth along with tomato paste, peanut butter, lentils, chickpeas, Sriracha, turmeric, and black pepper. Increase heat to medium-high and cover, but continue to stir frequently.

4. When the soup reaches a boil, reduce heat and allow to simmer for 20 minutes or until lentils, carrots, and squash are tender.

5. Stir in more broth or water if you prefer a thinner soup.

6. Serve with the optional garnishes and enjoy!

TYPE 2 DIABETES PREVENTION, TREATMENT, AND REVERSAL WITH A PLANT-BASED DIET

COLE ADAM, RD

The Centers for Disease Control and Prevention estimates that roughly half of U.S. adults are prediabetic or have type 2 diabetes.[31] This disease is characterized by insulin resistance, a state in which the body's response to insulin—a hormone that helps control blood glucose (sugar) levels—is impaired. Risk factors for type 2 diabetes include genetic predisposition, inactivity, and being overweight or obese, with the latter playing the biggest role.

As we accumulate body fat, it is deposited throughout our body. Although we may notice it more around our belly or legs, it also accumulates in our muscles (called intramyocellular lipid) and liver. When this occurs, the ability of our muscles and liver to respond to insulin is impaired by the fat cells, leading to a state of insulin resistance. This is problematic because muscle is one of our body's biggest users of glucose—pulling it from our blood and burning it for fuel or storing it for later. When glucose can't enter the muscle, it remains in the blood, leading to high blood glucose levels. A chronically elevated blood glucose level damages blood vessels and increases our risk for heart disease, blindness, kidney failure, amputations, infections, and premature death.

The good news is that type 2 diabetes is often preventable, treatable, and even reversible with a healthy diet and lifestyle. Maintaining a healthy body weight, staying active, and consuming a whole foods, plant-based diet are the best tools for preventing this disease. For those who already have type 2 diabetes, it has been shown that a low-fat, whole foods plant-based diet works *better* at improving blood glucose levels than a standard diabetic diet.[32,33] Eating legumes—beans, lentils, and split peas—appears to be especially beneficial. Legumes should be consumed with every meal, or at least on a daily basis. Their high fiber content slows the rate of carbohydrate digestion and absorption, blunting the post-meal spike in blood glucose.

In addition to a low-fat whole foods, plant-based diet, regular exercise has been shown to improve insulin sensitivity, helping to further lower blood glucose levels. And this combination of diet and exercise will also decrease body fat (including intramyocellular lipid), which drastically improves blood glucose levels. In fact, this effect can happen so quickly and be so powerful that if you are taking medication to manage your diabetes (especially insulin), you should inform your physician of these lifestyle changes. If these changes are made under your physician's supervision, they may be able to reduce or discontinue your diabetes medication![34,35]

GUT HEALTH AND A PLANT-BASED DIET

AUSTIN JOSEPH, WHOLE HEALTH CLUB NUTRITIONIST

Ninety-seven percent of people in the U.S. don't meet the recommended daily intake of fiber.[36] And with numbers like that, it's no wonder that we spend so much money in search of products and medications to help settle our stomachs, relieve constipation, and regulate our time on the toilet.

Could the answer really be as simple as more fiber? It may not solve everyone's digestive issues, but from what we've seen, more fiber has a *huge* impact on our clients' digestion and comfort! And fiber is *only* found in plants!

Fiber is critical to our gut health—the natural microflora (beneficial bacteria) in our intestines depend on it as a food source, and we have only recently started to understand just how important it is to keep these bacteria happy. In addition to simply making our digestive processes more regular, the types of bacteria that flourish when we take in more fiber have been shown to release beneficial compounds directly into our bloodstream. These compounds can help prevent diseases like arthritis and certain types of cancers.[37] They have also been shown to help improve immune system function.

Beneficial gut bacteria love foods rich in certain types of fibers, often called prebiotics. Different from probiotics, which contain actual live bacteria, prebiotics contain the nutrients needed to *feed* the communities of microflora in our intestines. Many staples in a plant-based diet are rich in these prebiotics, but if you really want to give your gut bacteria an edge, prioritize eating beans, onions, garlic, asparagus, leafy greens, and whole grains!

A happy, healthy gut means a happy, healthy you. Just remember that at the end of the day, the simplest way to love your gut bacteria (and make sure they'll love you back) is to eat more plants!

snacks

SPRING
ROLLS

YIELD: 24 ROLLS | COOK TIME: 20 MINUTES

INGREDIENTS:

1 PACK WONTON WRAPPERS (MAKE SURE THEY ARE EGG-FREE, WE LIKE FRIEDA'S BRAND)

1 ONION, DICED

1 CARROT, SLICED

2 CUPS OR ½ HEAD CABBAGE (GREEN OR PURPLE, CAN ALSO USE BOK CHOY)

3 GARLIC CLOVES, MINCED

1 TBSP. LOW-SODIUM VEGETABLE BROTH (FOR COOKING)

2 TSP. SESAME OIL

DIRECTIONS:

1. Preheat oven to 425 degrees Fahrenheit.

2. Sauté onions, carrots, and garlic with a splash of vegetable broth in a medium pan over medium-high heat.

3. Once onions start to become translucent, add in chopped cabbage.

4. Add in sesame oil and cook until veggies are soft. Remove from heat.

5. Spoon a thumb-sized amount of vegetable mixture onto a wonton wrapper. Wet edges of wonton wrapper and fold together the sides, pressing so the edges stick together. Repeat until you have used all of your filling and/or wonton wrappers.

6. Bake for 10-12 minutes or until wrappers are brown and crispy.

7. Dip in liquid aminos, coconut aminos or peanut sauce. (See recipe, page 17)

SUMMER
ROLLS

YIELD: 10-12 ROLLS | COOK TIME: 25 MINUTES

INGREDIENTS:

1 BLOCK EXTRA FIRM TOFU, DRAINED & PRESSED
2 TBSP. LIQUID AMINOS
2 TSP. GINGER POWDER
1 CUCUMBER
1 RED BELL PEPPER
1 CARROT
1 HEAD ROMAINE LETTUCE
1 PACK RICE PAPER
WARM WATER FOR SOAKING RICE PAPER
1 CUP FRESH BASIL
1 PACK RICE NOODLES
1 CUP CILANTRO OR PARSLEY, PULLED FROM STEMS

DIRECTIONS:

1. Preheat oven to 425 degrees Fahrenheit.

2. Cut tofu into long, thin strips. Lay out flat on a baking sheet and cover with liquid aminos and ginger powder. Bake for 15-20 minutes or until crispy.

3. Cook rice noodles according to package instructions. Drain & rinse, then set aside.

4. Julienne cucumber, bell pepper and carrot. Set aside.

5. Assemble spring rolls: take one piece of rice paper and soak it in warm water. Lay it flat and add a handful of rice noodles along with a few pieces of tofu, romaine, basil, cilantro or parsley and julienned veggies.

6. Tuck in the sides and roll the summer roll up until it seals (just like rolling a burrito).

7. Serve with peanut sauce. (see recipe, page 17)

DATE
BALLS

YIELD: 15-18 DATE BALLS | COOK TIME: 30 MINUTES

INGREDIENTS:

1 CUP NUTS (ALMONDS, CASHEWS, WALNUTS, OR PECANS)
2 CUPS PITTED DATES
1 TBSP. UNSWEETENED PLANT-BASED MILK OF CHOICE
2 TBSP. COCOA POWDER
1 TBSP. NUT BUTTER (ALMOND, PEANUT, OR CASHEW)
1 TSP. VANILLA
½ TSP. CINNAMON

TOPPINGS:
COCONUT FLAKES
MELTED ALMOND BUTTER
COCOA POWDER

DIRECTIONS:

1. Combine nuts and dates in a food processor and pulse until a thick dough mixture is formed.

2. Add in the rest of the ingredients and blend again until everything is well combined.

3. Pour mixture into a bowl and mix together with hands until dough can be molded into balls.

4. Using your hands or an ice cream scoop, roll out balls and place on a baking sheet lined with parchment paper or silicone baking mat.

5. Place in freezer for 30 minutes or in the fridge overnight to allow date balls to set.

ROASTED CHICKPEAS
3 WAYS

YIELD: 4 SERVINGS | COOK TIME: 25 MINUTES

INGREDIENTS:

WAY #1: SESAME GARLIC CHICKPEAS

1 CAN CHICKPEAS, DRAINED & RINSED

1 TBSP. SESAME OIL

2 TSP. GINGER POWDER

1 TBSP. GARLIC POWDER

½ TBSP. ONION POWDER

WAY #2: BBQ CHICKPEAS

1 CAN CHICKPEAS, DRAINED & RINSED

¼-½ CUP BBQ SAUCE OF CHOICE (SEE RECIPE ON PAGE 23 FOR HOMEMADE BBQ SAUCE)

WAY #3: SPICY BUFFALO CHICKPEAS

1 CAN CHICKPEAS, DRAINED & RINSED

¼-½ CUP FRANKS RED HOT SAUCE

¼ CUP NUTRITIONAL YEAST

DIRECTIONS:

1. Preheat oven to 425 degrees Fahrenheit.

2. Prepare chickpeas by tossing them in all spices or sauces under way #1, 2, or 3.

3. Place on a parchment-lined baking sheet, spreading them out so they cook evenly.

4. Bake in the oven for 15-20 minutes or until crispy. Cook longer to make them even more crispy, if preferred.

5. Let cool for 10 minutes, then remove from parchment paper and serve.

S P I N A C H
HUMMUS

YIELD: 4 SERVINGS | COOK TIME: 5 MINUTES

INGREDIENTS:

2 CANS CHICKPEAS, DRAINED & RINSED
¼ CUP TAHINI
3 GARLIC CLOVES
1 ½ LIMES, JUICED
2 CUPS FRESH SPINACH
2 TSP. BLACK PEPPER
½ CUP LOW-SODIUM VEGETABLE BROTH
1 TBSP. CUMIN
1 TBSP. ONION POWDER

DIRECTIONS:

1. Combine all ingredients in a food processor or blender.

2. Blend until smooth. Add more vegetable broth to thin hummus if needed.

3. Taste and adjust seasoning if needed.

K A L E
CHIPS

YIELD: 1-2 | COOK TIME: 45 MINUTES

INGREDIENTS:

1 BUNCH GREEN KALE, DE-STEMMED, TORN INTO CHIP-SIZE PIECES, RINSED,
AND DRIED (MAKE SURE IT'S COMPLETELY DRY)
¾ CUP RAW UNSALTED CASHEWS, SOAKED IN WATER FOR AT LEAST TWO HOURS AND DRAINED
3 TBSP. APPLE CIDER VINEGAR
1 LEMON, JUICED
¼ CUP NUTRITIONAL YEAST
6-7 GARLIC CLOVES
½ TBSP. MAPLE SYRUP OR AGAVE NECTAR
½ TSP. TURMERIC
¼ TSP. BLACK PEPPER

DIRECTIONS:

1. Preheat oven to 225 degrees Fahrenheit.

2. Add everything except the kale to a food processor and purée.

3. Transfer the purée to a large bowl and add kale to the bowl.

4. Massage the purée into the kale pieces, coating evenly.

5. Spread the kale in a single layer over 2-3 large baking sheets.

6. Bake for 30 minutes or until the kale is crispy. If there are still a few soggy pieces
    after 30 minutes, remove the crispy pieces and put the soggy ones back in the oven
    until they're crispy.

POTATO
WEDGES

YIELD: 3-4 SERVINGS | COOK TIME: 40 MINUTES

INGREDIENTS:

5 RUSSET POTATOES
2 TSP. BLACK PEPPER
2 TBSP. LOW-SODIUM VEGETABLE BROTH

OPTIONAL TOPPINGS
PARSLEY FOR GARNISH
KETCHUP FOR DIPPING

DIRECTIONS:

1. Preheat oven to 400 degrees Fahrenheit.

2. Wash potatoes and cut into long wedges. Lay out on a baking sheet lined with parchment paper or a silicon baking mat.

3. Transfer potatoes to a bowl and toss in vegetable broth. Sprinkle black pepper over potatoes and mix together to coat evenly.

4. Bake potatoes in oven for 30-35 minutes or until brown and crispy. Allow to cool for 5-10 minutes before serving.

TOMATO BALSAMIC SALAD
WITH TOFU FETA

YIELD: 3-4 SERVINGS | COOK TIME: 5 MINUTES

INGREDIENTS:

2 CUPS MULTI-COLORED CHERRY TOMATOES, CUT IN HALF
½ BLOCK TOFU, DRAINED AND PRESSED
¼ RED ONION, DICED
2 TBSP. BALSAMIC VINEGAR
1 TBSP. FRESH BASIL, CHOPPED
1 TBSP. NUTRITIONAL YEAST
2 TSP. DRIED OREGANO
1 TSP. BLACK PEPPER
1 TSP. GARLIC POWDER

DIRECTIONS:

1. Cut pressed tofu into small cubes.

2. Toss tofu in a bowl with fresh basil, nutritional yeast, oregano, black pepper and garlic powder. Be careful not to crush the tofu as you mix in the spices.

3. Add in tomato halves and red onions.

4. Sprinkle in balsamic vinegar. Eat as is or refrigerate overnight.

CHICKPEA
NUGGETS

YIELD: 15-18 NUGGETS | COOK TIME: 40 MINUTES

INGREDIENTS:

1 CAN CHICKPEAS, DRAINED AND RINSED
1 ONION, DICED
2 CARROTS, DICED
3 GARLIC CLOVES
½ CUP NUTRITIONAL YEAST
1 TBSP. SMOKED PAPRIKA
1 TBSP. CUMIN
2 TBSP. OREGANO
2 TSP. BASIL
2 TSP. BLACK PEPPER
2 CUPS BREADCRUMBS
½ CUP OATS

DIRECTIONS:

1. Preheat oven to 350 degrees Fahrenheit.

2. Pulse chickpeas in a food processor until they are mashed but still chunky. Set aside, leaving them in the food processor.

3. Heat a medium pan over medium heat. Once hot, add onions, carrots, garlic and a splash of vegetable broth. Sauté until onions are translucent, then add in nutritional yeast and spices.

4. Transfer mixture from the pan to the food processor and blend until everything is combined with the chickpeas.

5. Pour mixture into a bowl and stir in breadcrumbs and oats. Mix until you get a dough thick enough to form balls with.

6. Form nuggets with your hands and lay out on a parchment-lined baking sheet.

7. Bake for 15 minutes. Flip nuggets over and bake again for 5-10 minutes until nuggets are golden brown and crispy on all sides.

AVOCADO TOAST
3 WAYS

YIELD: 2-4 PIECES OF TOAST | COOK TIME: 5 MINUTES

INGREDIENTS:

WAY #1: KALAMATA OLIVE TOAST
2 LARGE RIPE AVOCADOS
2-4 PIECES SOURDOUGH BREAD
KALAMATA OLIVE SPREAD
1 ROMA TOMATO, DICED

WAY #2: RED PEPPER AVOCADO TOAST
2 LARGE RIPE AVOCADOS
2-4 PIECES SOURDOUGH BREAD
½ TSP. RED PEPPER FLAKES
2 TBSP. FRESH LEMON JUICE

WAY #3: GARDEN RADISH AVOCADO TOAST
2 LARGE RIPE AVOCADOS
2-4 PIECES SOURDOUGH BREAD
1 SMALL HANDFUL BROCCOLI SPROUTS
1 RADISH, SLICED THINLY
2 TBSP. FRESH LEMON JUICE

DIRECTIONS:

1. Toast bread until golden brown.

2. Slice and remove pits from avocados. Place into a medium bowl and mash with a fork or potato masher.

3. Spread avocado mash on toasted bread.

   Kalamata Olive Toast: Layer Kalamata Olive spread on top of avocado spread.

   Red Pepper Avocado Toast: sprinkle red pepper flakes over avocados and top with lemon juice.

   Garden Radish Avocado Toast: distribute a handful of broccoli sprouts evenly over top of avocado toast. Top with sliced radish and lemon juice.

MINDFUL EATING 101

COLE ADAM, RD

Have you ever devoured a whole bag of popcorn before the movie even starts? Or inhaled lunch while scrolling through your phone? And haven't we all polished off a pint of ice cream after a bad day? These examples are the epitome of *mindless* eating, which is the exact opposite of *mindful* eating. Engaging in mindful eating can help people lose weight and improve disordered eating patterns. It also encourages a healthy relationship with food.

The phrase "mindful eating" is an umbrella term for a variety of behavior changes that can improve our relationship with food. Here are the most common strategies we can implement to eat more mindfully:

- **Slow down:** Eating too fast can override satiety signals, which may lead to overeating. Some tricks to help slow down while eating include: setting the fork/spoon down in between bites, engaging in conversation while eating (in-person, not on the phone), and not scooping up another mouthful until you've thoroughly chewed and swallowed the previous one.
- **Avoid distractions:** Avoid eating while watching TV, reading, driving, or being on the phone or computer. A distracted eater is more likely to overeat, get less pleasure from the food they are eating, and eat too fast. Ideally, we should consume meals while sitting down at a table. A bonus is having a good old-fashioned family meal, as this has been shown to have a positive impact on school performance and social skills in children.
- **Know the difference between physical and emotional hunger:** Physical hunger comes from the body/stomach and represents true hunger. Emotional hunger comes from our mind and may be caused by stress, anger, boredom, loneliness, or anxiety. Before eating, identify the source of hunger. Is this true physical hunger, or is it just stress or boredom? If it's true physical hunger, then eat. If not, identify the cause of emotional hunger and address that instead.

- **Pay attention to satiety cues:** In Okinawa, Japan—a Blue Zone that boasts one of the longest life expectancies in the world—those following a traditional diet often recite the mantra "hara hachi bu" before eating, which translates to "Eat until you are 80% full." While these Okinawan elders aren't calculating their exact fullness percentage while eating, the practice reminds them to stop eating when full, which prevents them from overeating.
- **Eat foods that nourish:** The saying "you are what you eat" is reasonably accurate. The cells and tissues in our bodies are constantly being broken down and rebuilt, and the main building blocks are nutrients from our diets. When we consume a nutrient-dense diet rich in whole plant-based foods, we provide our bodies with the best raw materials to maintain and fuel themselves. Shifting our state of mind from "food only provides pleasure" to "food nourishes, fuels, and heals," can help us make healthier decisions about what we choose to eat.

RETHINKING CONVENIENCE FOODS

AUSTIN JOSEPH, WHC NUTRITIONIST

We've all been too short on time to prepare a full meal. Maybe your lunch break gets cut short and you only have five minutes to make something happen, so you grab a bag of chips from the vending machine. Or maybe your evening schedule sounds something like this: pick up your three kids from school at 3:15 PM, take them to soccer practice, piano lessons, or study group at 4:00, 4:30, and 5:15, respectively. Turn back around and pick them up at 5:30, 6:00, and 7:10, and somehow get everyone home before the dog pees on the carpet. On a night like that, you don't have time to cook a family dinner, but you *do* have time to swing through the nearest drive-through.

The problem is, all those bags of chips and drive-through trips take a serious toll on our health. We need to find a better way to use our limited time if we're going to make a positive change for ourselves. Luckily, we can unlearn the drive-through reflex and train ourselves to use that time for a healthier purpose. We need to rethink what convenience foods really mean—and whether "convenience" really needs to mean "unhealthy."

Five minutes for lunch could mean a bag of chips, or you could go for one of our favorite quick snacks: a simple can of chickpeas emptied into a bowl, splashed with hot sauce, and microwaved for two minutes. Is it a gourmet meal? Nope. But it's more filling, lower in calories, higher in nutrients, and better for our bodies than a bag of chips. As long as you can remember to bring a few items like canned chickpeas and sauce for use in a kitchenette (or even just a bunch of fruit for something really simple), you can set yourself up for success while you're short on time.

Likewise, you could throw together a quick cooler full of flatbread, tofu, veggies, and hummus (or even ingredients for a simple peanut butter & jelly) for the kids to make wraps or sandwiches in the car on the way to your busy evening's various activities. It'll take practice and a mindset shift to switch to that from a drive-through, but it takes about the same amount of time and provides a much more nutritious meal for the family!

Here are a few tips to set yourself up for success

- **Prep staples when you have time:** if you have tofu cubes, rice, or other staples cooked and ready to go in your fridge, you can reheat them and combine them with a few other ingredients in a matter of seconds.

- **Recognize patterns and plan ahead:** if you know the meeting every Monday always runs into your lunch break, plan to have only five minutes for lunch on Mondays! Show up to work with a pre-prepped meal, an arm full of fresh fruit, or your trusty can of chickpeas and bottle of hot sauce.

- **Practice makes perfect:** while these switches might be simple, learning to do them instead of falling into old habits takes time and practice. Don't get discouraged if you find yourself having a hard time with ideas for your new "convenience" foods. The longer you're doing it, the easier it'll get!

smoothies

C H O C O L A T E
FROSTY

YIELD: 1 SMOOTHIE | COOK TIME: 5 MINUTES

INGREDIENTS:

1 FROZEN RIPE BANANA

4 MEDJOOL DATES, PITTED

2 TBSP. CACAO OR COCOA POWDER

1-2 TBSP. NATURAL PEANUT BUTTER (OPTIONAL)

½ SCOOP VANILLA PLANT-BASED PROTEIN POWDER (OPTIONAL)

1-2 HANDFULS ICE CUBES

1-2 CUPS UNSWEETENED PLANT-BASED MILK OF CHOICE

DIRECTIONS:

1. Place all ingredients in the order listed in a high speed blender and blend until smooth.

    Tip: *We recommend keeping several bananas peeled and frozen at all times so they're ready to go for smoothies!*

PUMPKIN SPICE
SMOOTHIE

YIELD 1-2 SMOOTHIES | COOK TIME: 5 MINUTES

INGREDIENTS:

1 FROZEN RIPE BANANA
½ CUP CANNED PUMPKIN PUREE
4 PITTED DATES
1 TBSP. HEMP SEEDS
2 TBSP. PUMPKIN PIE SPICE BLEND
½ TSP. VANILLA EXTRACT
1-2 HANDFULS ICE CUBES
1-2 CUPS UNSWEETENED PLANT-BASED MILK OF CHOICE

DIRECTIONS:

1. Place all ingredients in the order listed in a high speed blender and blend until smooth.

S U P E R F O O D
SMOOTHIE

INGREDIENTS:

1 FROZEN RIPE BANANA

2 CUPS FROZEN MIXED BERRIES

½ CUP GRAPES OR PITTED CHERRIES

½ CUP FROZEN CHOPPED KALE OR PACKED FRESH KALE

1 TBSP. HEMP OR CHIA SEEDS

1-2 HANDFULS ICE CUBES

1 CUP UNSWEETENED PLANT-BASED MILK OF CHOICE

1 CUP WATER

DIRECTIONS:

1. De-stem kale if using fresh kale

2. Place all ingredients in the order listed in a high speed blender and blend until smooth.

THE GREEN
MONSTER

YIELD: 1-2 SMOOTHIES | COOK TIME: 5 MINUTES

INGREDIENTS:

1 FROZEN RIPE BANANA

1 ½ CUPS FROZEN DICED MANGO (SET OUT TO THAW FOR A FEW MINUTES)

2 CUPS THAWED FROZEN CHOPPED KALE OR PACKED FRESH KALE

1 TBSP. PUMPKIN SEEDS

½ SCOOP VANILLA PLANT-BASED PROTEIN POWDER (OPTIONAL)

1-2 HANDFULS ICE CUBES

1 CUP UNSWEETENED PLANT-BASED MILK OF CHOICE

1 CUP WATER

DIRECTIONS:

1. De-stem kale if using fresh kale

2. Place all ingredients in the order listed in a high speed blender and blend until smooth.

REVITALIZING TROPICAL
SMOOTHIE

YIELD: 1-2 SMOOTHIES | COOK TIME: 5 MINUTES

INGREDIENTS:

1 FROZEN RIPE BANANA

1 NAVEL ORANGE, PEELED (YOU CAN SUB A PEACH OR NECTARINE DEPENDING ON THE SEASON)

1 CARROT, CHOPPED OR SHREDDED

1 ½ CUPS FROZEN MANGO, SLIGHTLY THAWED

1 TBSP. HEMP SEEDS

½ TSP. GROUND TURMERIC

1 TSP. GROUND GINGER

A PINCH OF GROUND BLACK PEPPER

1-2 HANDFULS ICE CUBES

1 CUP WATER

DIRECTIONS:

1. Place all ingredients in the order listed in a high speed blender and blend until smooth.

ALL ABOUT PHYTOCHEMICALS

COLE ADAM, RD

Phytochemicals are compounds made by plants (*phyto* means plant in Greek). They're produced to protect plants from diseases, pathogens, and predators. Fortunately for us, these phytochemicals are also beneficial nutrients and account for many of the reasons plants protect our health.

Thousands of phytochemicals have been identified, and there are probably more we haven't discovered yet. Some of the more well-known phytochemicals include lycopene, found in tomatoes, and beta-carotene, found in orange produce such as carrots and butternut squash. Other phytochemicals include anthocyanins, found in berries, and sulforaphane in broccoli and cabbage.

Phytochemicals are considered non-essential nutrients (since we won't immediately die without them), but a growing pool of research suggests that they play a vital role in keeping us healthy. They can serve as antioxidants, mimic certain hormones, manipulate enzymes, and influence DNA replication. Through these actions, phytochemicals have been shown to prevent cell damage, prevent cancer formation, slow or inhibit cancer growth, strengthen immune function, fight viruses, reduce inflammation, promote the body's detoxification enzymes, and protect us from DNA damage.

Phytochemicals are found *only* in plants and are often responsible for the color, flavor, and scents of plants. Although all plant-based foods contain phytochemicals, some contain more than others. Here's a list of the top phytochemical-rich food groups:

- Cruciferous vegetables (broccoli, cabbage, cauliflower, brussels sprouts)
- Dark leafy green vegetables (kale, spinach, collard greens, arugula)
- Berries (blueberries, raspberries, blackberries, cranberries, strawberries)
- Soybeans and soy products (tofu, edamame, tempeh, soy milk)
- Other legumes (black beans, lentils, split peas)
- Whole grains (rice, buckwheat, oats, whole wheat, corn)
- Allium vegetables (garlic, onions, shallots, leeks)
- Other fruit (grapes, cherries, cantaloupe, apricots, apples, plums, oranges)
- Other vegetables (sweet potatoes, carrots, tomatoes, peppers)

- Beverages (green tea, coffee, herbal teas)
- Herbs and spices (turmeric, cinnamon, cloves, ginger, basil, parsley, oregano, mint)

To reap the health benefits of phytochemicals, we should make an extra effort to include the foods listed above in our diet. As previously mentioned, phytochemicals are responsible for the color of many foods—they're what make blueberries blue and oranges orange—so a great way to ensure we're loading up on as many phytochemicals as possible is to eat a variety of naturally colorful foods!

CANCER PREVENTION

COLE ADAM, RD

It's largely assumed that genetics are the most important factor in determining whether or not we develop cancer. While this is still up for debate, we are of the opinion that *controllable* risk factors are the ones we should focus on the most. After all, while factors like genetics are important for detection, focusing on controllable risk factors can help us actually mitigate our risk. We prefer to focus on the ways we can help improve our odds rather than dwelling on something out of our control.

Tobacco and alcohol consumption, excessive sun exposure, a lack of exercise, red and processed meat consumption, and obesity all *increase* our risk of developing cancer. On the other hand, avoiding or minimizing these risk factors—along with maintaining a healthy body weight, regular exercise, and a healthy diet—can significantly *lower* our risk of developing cancer.[38]

Research on the role of diet in cancer prevention strongly suggests that a diet centered on unprocessed plant foods such as whole grains, legumes, fruits, vegetables, nuts, and seeds is our best dietary strategy for cancer prevention. This aligns with the dietary recommendations from the American Cancer Society.[39] The following foods appear especially protective against cancer:

- Cruciferous vegetables such as broccoli, cauliflower, cabbage, and Brussels sprouts.
- Allium vegetables such as garlic, onions, shallots, and leeks.
- All varieties of edible mushrooms.
- Dark leafy greens such as kale, spinach, arugula, and collard greens.

- Orange produce such as carrots, sweet potatoes, butternut squash, and apricots.
- Nuts and seeds, especially flaxseeds and walnuts.
- All varieties of berries and citrus fruit.
- Green tea and coffee (without added cream or sugar).
- All types of spices and herbs, especially ginger and turmeric.
- All varieties of legumes (beans, split peas, lentils), especially minimally processed soy products like tofu, tempeh, edamame, and soy milk.

These foods work to protect us from cancer through various mechanisms. Most are rich in antioxidants, which help prevent DNA damage and keep us healthy on a cellular level. Some contain unique compounds that have been shown to inhibit cancer cell growth. Others influence our hormones, keeping them in normal ranges. Regardless of the specific mechanism, these foods are well-established as potent anti-cancer foods. We should make an extra effort to include them in our diet on a regular basis.

LAST THOUGHTS

We hope you've enjoyed and found useful the recipes and information presented in this book. We're confident that the more you incorporate this way of eating into your life, the healthier you'll be and the better you'll feel. Combine this diet with other healthy lifestyle behaviors, and you'll be unstoppable! Here are some well-established practices that can boost health and happiness:

- Make sure to be active every day. The best form of exercise is whatever you enjoy doing. Anything that gets your body up and moving is beneficial, so whether it's ballroom dancing or kickboxing, go for it! In addition to structured exercise, stay active and moving throughout the day with low-impact movements such as walking, gardening, or stretching. Avoid sitting for long periods of time.
- Fully engage in your life. Be socially active, try new things, get out and see the world. Instead of sitting in your living room watching TV, go for a hike, see a movie with a friend, host a game night, attend a lecture, visit a museum, or check out a sporting event. Stay curious and never stop learning.
- Find ways to minimize or manage stress. Exercise is a great way to lower stress. Other proven methods include meditation, restorative

yoga, getting a massage, spending time in nature, spending time with animals, laughing, and being socially active. Although it's great to be active and engaged in life, you should also find time to unwind and relax. Curl up with a good book, soak in a hot bath, or take an afternoon catnap with your cat.

- Sleep well. Adequate sleep is essential for good health, especially brain health. Adults should aim for at least seven hours per night. Some strategies to promote good sleep include having consistent sleep/wake times, making your sleep environment cool, quiet, and dark, avoiding screens and bright lights during the 1-2 hours before bedtime; and avoiding caffeine after noon.

- Find a healthy community! Building a group of friends that will exercise or eat healthy foods with you is key to maintaining your healthy lifestyle. We'd love to have you stay in touch with our community! You can join us on Facebook at Whole Health Club or on Instagram at @wholehealthclub. You can also find us at www.wholehealthclub.com.

Most people want to live a long, happy, and healthy life. Adopting a plant-based diet and other healthy lifestyle behaviors will put you in the best possible position to do just that. As the saying goes, "Health is wealth." Invest wisely.

Cheers!

Kayla, Cole, and Austin

REFERENCES

1. Ornish D, Scherwitz LW, Billings JH. "Intensive Lifestyle Changes for Reversal of Coronary Artery Disease." *JAMA.* December 1998. https://doi.org/10.1001/jama.280.23.2001

2. Zalvan Craig H. MD et al. "A Comparison of Alkaline Water and Mediterranean Diet vs Proton Pump Inhibition for Treatment of Laryngopharyngeal Reflux" *JAMA Otolaryngol Head Neck Surg.* October 2017. https://doi.org/10.1001/jamaoto.2017.1454

3. Siener R, Hesse A. "The effect of a vegetarian and different omnivorous diets on urinary risk factors for uric acid stone formation." *European Journal of Nutrition.* December 2003. https://doi.org/10.1007/s00394-003-0428-0

4. Chiba Mitsuro et al. "Lifestyle-related disease in Crohn's disease: Relapse prevention by a semi-vegetarian diet." *World Journal of Gastroenterology.* May 2010. https://doi.org/10.3748/wjg.v16.i20.2484

5. Esposito K et al. "Mediterranean diet improves erectile function in subjects with the metabolic syndrome." *International Journal of Impotence Research.* July-August 2006. https://doi.org/10.1038/sj.ijir.3901447

6. Campbell, Thomas. "A plant-based diet and stroke." *Journal of Geriatric Cardiology.* May 2017. https://doi.org/10.11909/j.issn.1671-5411.2017.05.010

7. Mazidi M, Pascal Kegne A. "Higher adherence to plant-based diets are associated with lower likelihood of fatty liver" *Clinical Nutrition.* August 2019. https://doi.org/10.1016/j.clnu.2018.08.010

8. Tracy CR et al. "Animal protein and the risk of kidney stones: a comparative metabolic study of animal protein sources." *Journal of Urology.* July 2014. https://doi.org/10.1016/j.juro.2014.01.093

9. Chun-Ming Chang et al. "Plant-based diet, Cholesterol, and Risk of Gallstone Disease: A Prospective Study." *Nutrients.* February 2019. https://doi.org/10.3390/nu11020335

10. Hever, Julieanna. "Plant-based Diets: A Physician's Guide." *The Permanente Journal.* Summer 2016. https://doi.org/10.7812/TPP/15-082

11. "Livestock's Long Shadow." Food and Agriculture Organization of the United Nations. 2006. Accessed August 19, 2019. http://www.fao.org/3/a0701e/a0701e00.htm

12. "History of Blue Zones," Blue Zones, accessed June 18, 2018, https://www.blue-zones.com/about/history/

13. "Food Guidelines," Blue Zones, accessed June 18, 2018, https://www.bluezones.com/recipes/food-guidelines/

14. "Power 9® Reverse Engineering Longevity," Blue Zones, accessed June 18, 2018, https://www.bluezones.com/2016/11/power-9/

15. Rueda-Clausen CF, Silva FA, Lindarte MA, Villa-Roel C, Gomez E, Gutierrez R, Cure-Cure C, López-Jaramillo P. "Olive, soybean and palm oils intake have a similar acute detrimental effect over the endothelial function in healthy young subjects." *Nutrition, Metabolism & Cardiovascular Diseases* (January 2007) https://doi.org/10.1016/j.numecd.2005.08.008

16. Michael Greger, "If Fructose is Bad, What about Fruit?" NutritionFacts.org, Accessed June 4, 2017, https://nutritionfacts.org/video/if-fructose-is-bad-what-about-fruit/

17. Törrönen R, Kolehmainen M, Sarkkinen E, Poutanen K, Mykkänen H, Niskanen L. "Berries reduce postprandial insulin responses to wheat and rye breads in healthy women." *The Journal of Nutrition.* (April 2017), https://doi.org/10.3945/jn.112.169771

18. Budhathoki S, et al. "Association of Animal and Plant Protein Intake With All-Cause and Cause-Specific Mortality" *JAMA Intern Med.* August 2019. https://doi.org/10.1001/jamainternmed.2019.2806

19. Yusuf S et al. "Effect of Potentially Modifiable Risk Factors Associated with Myocardial Infarction in 52 Countries (the INTERHEART study): case-control study." *The Lancet* (September 2004). https://doi.org/10.1016/S0140-6736(04)17018-9

20. Esselstyn CB Jr, Gendy G, Doyle J, Golubic M, Roizen MF. "A Way to Reverse CAD?" *Journal of Family Practice* (July 2014). https://www.ncbi.nlm.nih.gov/pubmed/25198208

21. Fung TT, Willett WC, Stampfer MJ, Manson JE, Hu FB. "Dietary Patterns and the Risk of Coronary Heart Disease in Women." *Arch Intern Med* (2001). https://doi.org/10.1001/archinte.161.15.1857

22. Frank B Hu, Eric B Rimm, Meir J Stampfer, Alberto Ascherio, Donna Spiegelman, Walter C Willett. "Prospective study of major dietary patterns and risk of coronary heart disease in men." *The American Journal of Clinical Nutrition* (October 2000). https://doi.org/10.1093/ajcn/72.4.912

23. Iris Erlund, Raika Koli, Georg Alfthan, Jukka Marniemi, Pauli Puukka, Pirjo Mustonen, Pirjo Mattila, Antti Jula, "Favorable effects of berry consumption on platelet function, blood pressure, and HDL cholesterol." *The American Journal of Clinical Nutrition* (February 2008). https://doi.org/10.1093/ajcn/87.2.323

24. Huang, H. et al. "Effects of Berries Consumption on Cardiovascular Risk Factors: A Meta-analysis with Trial Sequential Analysis of Randomized Controlled Trials." *Scientific Reports* (2016). https://doi.org/10.1038/srep23625

25. Sindi, Shireen et al. "Healthy Dietary Changes in Midlife Are Associated with Reduced Dementia Risk Later in Life." *Nutrients* (Nov. 2018) https://doi.org10.3390/nu10111649

26. Ondine van de Rest, Agnes AM Berendsen, Annemien Haveman-Nies, Lisette CPGM de Groot. "Dietary Patterns, Cognitive Decline, and Dementia: A Systematic Review." *Advances in Nutrition* (March 2015). https://doi.org/10.3945/an.114.007617

27. Pistollato, F et al. "Nutritional patterns associated with the maintenance of neuro-cognitive functions and the risk of dementia and Alzheimer's disease: A focus on human studies." *Pharmacological Research* (May 2018). https://doi.org/10.1016/j.phrs.2018.03.012

28. Nilsson A, Salo I, Plaza M, Björck I. "Effects of a mixed berry beverage on cognitive functions and cardiometabolic risk markers; A randomized cross-over study in healthy older adults." *Plos One* (2017). https://doi.org/10.1371/journal.pone.0188173

29. Subash, Selvaraju et al. "Neuroprotective effects of berry fruits on neurodegenerative diseases." *Neural Regeneration Research* (2014). https://doi.org/10.4103/1673-5374.139483

30. Morris MC, Yang Y, Barnes LL, Bennett DA, Dawson-Hughes B, Booth SL. "Nutrients and Bioactives in Green Leafy Vegetables and Cognitive Decline: Prospective Study." *Neurology* (January 2018), https://doi.org/10.1212/WNL.0000000000004815

31. "National Diabetes Statistics Report, 2017." Centers for Disease Control and Prevention. 2017. Accessed September 37, 2018. https://www.cdc.gov/diabetes/data/statistics-report/index.html

32. Barnard ND et al. "A Low-fat Vegan Diet Improves Glycemic Control and Cardiovascular Risk Factors in a Randomized Clinical Trial in Individuals with Type 2 Diabetes." *Diabetes Care* (August 2006), https://doi.org/10.2337/dc06-0606

33. Barnard ND et al. "A Low-fat Vegan Diet and a Conventional Diabetes Diet in the Treatment of Type 2 Diabetes: a Randomized, Controlled, 74-wk Clinical Trial." *American Journal of Clinical Nutrition* (May 2009), https://doi.org/10.3945/ajcn.2009.26736H

34. Barnard, RJ et al. "Diet and exercise in the treatment of NIDDM. The need for early emphasis." *Diabetes Care* (Dec 1994). https://doi.org/10.2337/diacare.17.12.1469

35. Kahleova, H et al. "Vegetarian diet improves insulin resistance and oxidative stress markers more than conventional diet in subjects with Type 2 diabetes." *Diabetic medicine: a journal of the British Diabetic Association* (2011). https://doi.org/10.1111/j.1464-5491.2010.03209.x

36. Moshfegh A, Goldman J, Cleveland L. *What We Eat in America.* NHANES 2001-2002: Usual Nutrient Intakes from Food Compared to Dietary Reference Intakes. U.S. Department of Agriculture, Agricultural Research Service. 2005. Accessed June 2, 2019. https://www.ars.usda.gov/ARSUserFiles/80400530/pdf/0102/usualintaketables2001-02.pdf

37. "Can Gut Bacteria Help Improve Your Health? Initial research suggests certain bacteria in your gut can prevent and treat many common diseases." *Harvard Men's Health Watch.* Harvard Medical School. October 2016. Accessed June 2, 2019. https://www.health.harvard.edu/staying-healthy/can-gut-bacteria-improve-your-health

38. McKenzie, Fiona et al. "Healthy Lifestyle and Risk of Cancer in the European Prospective Investigation Into Cancer and Nutrition Cohort Study." *Medicine* (2016). https://doi.org/10.1097/MD.0000000000002850

39. "Summary of the ACS Guidelines on Nutrition and Physical Activity." American Cancer Society. February 2016. Accessed September 29, 2019.

IMAGES

Physical Map of the World. Digital Image. Free Physical Maps of the World, Mapswire.com. 2018. Accessed June 19, 2018. Labeled for Commercial Reuse with Modification.

Pexels. Food Prep Kitchen. Digital Image. Pixabay.com. December 31, 2012. October 11, 2019. Pixabay License, Free for Commercial Use.

Buissinne, Steve. *Olive Oil.* Digital Image. Pixabay.com. October 5, 2015. August 4, 2019. Pixabay License, Free for Commercial Use.

Silvia. *Salad.* Digital Image. Pixabay.com. September 16, 2016. August 4, 2019. Pixabay License, Free for Commercial Use.

Grantham, Sam. Joseph, Austin. *WHC Eating Chart.* Digital Image. Whole Health Club. Accessed August 15, 2018. Used with permission of Whole Health Club.

Leone, Ulrike. *Beans.* Digital Image. Pixabay.com. January 26, 2018. Accessed September 14, 2019. Pixabay License, Free for Commercial Use.